Combustible Demand-Sensitive Automobile Flow Management Coordination and Path Selection in Automobile Infrastructureless Environments

Lucian

Combustible Demand-Sensitive Automobile Flow Management Coordination and Path Selection in Automobile Infrastructureless Environments

First Edition June 2025

Written by Lucian

TABLE OF CONTENTS

CHAPTER NO.		TITLE		PAGE NO.

CHAPTER 1

INTRODUCTION

1.1 OVERVIEW OF VEHICULAR ADHOC NETWORK

Transportation system holds a huge importance among policy makers, researchers, and automobile manufacturers recently (Sumalee & Ho 2018). The rising traffic congestions, injuries and mortalities in road accidents have rendered to be one among the world's biggest "public health" and "injury prevention" issue. The death rate in the entire world is nearly 1.25 million yearly from just road accidents. Young people in the age group 15-29 years are more susceptible to death owing to rising road traffic injuries. As per the third Global status report issued on road safety, it has been predicted that the low and middle income nations contribute towards 90% of the world's injury rate resulting in 3% GDP on road traffic accidents. According to the Government of India, Transport Research Wing (TRW) of Ministry of Transport and Highways, the overall number of road fatal conditions rose by 2.5% from 4,89,400 in 2014 to 5,01,423 in 2015. There is also a rise in the overall number of death and injuries in road accidents by 4.6% and 1.4% correspondingly between 2014 and 2015. (Mortality Rate: 1,39,671 in 2014 to 1,46,133 in 2015, while Injury rate: 4,93,474 in 2014 to 5,00,279 in 2015). In India, daily nearly 1,374 accidents and 400 deaths occur which again changes into 57 accidents and 17 fatalities on road each hour on an average.

Currently, road accidents constitute the 9th important reason behind the death worldwide across all age groups. By the year 2030, it will further move to the 7th prominent reason behind death in case not enough prevention measures and actions are adopted (Rus *et al.* 2019). Since the traffic crashes are both assumable and avoidable, the World Health Organization (WHO) in coordination with United Nations General Assembly in 2010 has made a resolution resulting in the establishment of the Decade of Action for Road Safety (2011-2020). Also, the focus towards road safety has been also identified in 2030 Sustainable Development agenda. India is also answerable to Brasilia Declaration to accomplish the objective of this agenda. The goal of this agenda is to accomplish 50% decrease in road mortality by 2020 which will hugely affect both health and environment universally. (Source: WHO, 2013 statistics). Hence, the concept of so known "Intelligent Transportation System" (ITS) was highlighted to encourage the road safety and reduce the impacts of congestions, accidents and crashes.

ITS brought in Information Technology to the vehicles so that driving can become safer, streamlined and cozy (Canavari *et al.* 2016). Therefore, vehicular communication network evolved to facilitate a communication web among vehicles and road side structures. This vehicular communication allows the 'fully connected', 'information–abundant', 'fast' and 'cost effective' data distribution so that safety, comfort, and urban awareness of the passengers are fulfilled and the adverse environmental effects are reduced. As per 2011, Applications for the Environment: Real-time Information Synthesis (AERIS) report published by U.S. Department of Transportation; the ITS strategies that has been highlighted consists of adaptive cruise control (ACC), eco-driving help, and eco-routing, which try to have an influence on the driving behaviour in a way that helps to decrease the emissions on the whole. It also consists of traffic management and control tactics, which is used in the dynamic management of the traffic, decreases the congestion, re-routes the traffic, and thus, reduces the fuel usage and overall generation of expulsions.

Vehicular Ad-hoc Network is regarded to be a special group of Mobile Ad-hoc networks (MANET) comprising of several vehicles capable of communicating with one another with no static infrastructure (Kumar & Chhabra 2016). Here, vehicles can communicate with one another in the moving vehicles, static infrastructure and road-side unit (RSU) to satisfy the passenger's safety, problems and comfort. Vehicles communicate with the rest of the moving vehicles close by, since it provides support to a hugely dynamic network topology with ultra speed, self-configuration and decentralized restraints. VANET enables short to medium range wireless communication (approx. 1000m) among vehicles, infrastructure and RSUs utilizing Dedicated Short-range Communication (DSRC) protocol. Federal Communication Commission (FCC) of US assigned 75 MHz of bandwidth in the 5.9 GHz (5.85-5.925 GHz) band for the DSRC generation. DSRC standard enables the overall safety and efficacy of the transportation system by connecting the unformidable technology of wireless communication among vehicular web. Hence, DSRC is also called as WAVE (Wireless Access in Vehicular Environments) in which it facilitates vehicular communication at lesser latency having a higher data transfer rate (up to 27Mbps) with no charges for usage. In addition, WAVE falls under IEEE 1609 protocol, employs a new amendment of IEEE 802.11 standard i.e. IEEE 802.11p standard to provide support to vehicular networking communication.

1.1.1 VANET Architecture

Organizations such as IEEE, ISO and C2C-CC have recommended VANETs architecture, which differs between regions. The IEEE presented WAVE for single hop, unicast vehicular communication employing DSRC (Rasheed *et al.* 2017). On the other side, ISO's prosed CALM i.e. Continuous Air Interface for Long to Medium Range supports unicast and also broadcast communication among vehicles and between vehicles and road infrastructure. European car industry introduced the Car-to-Car Consortium (C2C-CC) that emerged the primary driving strength behind Vehicular Communication in 2007. It concentrates on Car to Car multi-hop and geo-networking applying DSRC and other WLAN standards. The communication modes of C2C-CC include unicast, broadcast, geo-unicast and geo-broadcast. Figure 1.1 shows the C2C-CC architecture, which includes in-vehicle, ad-hoc and infrastructure domains.

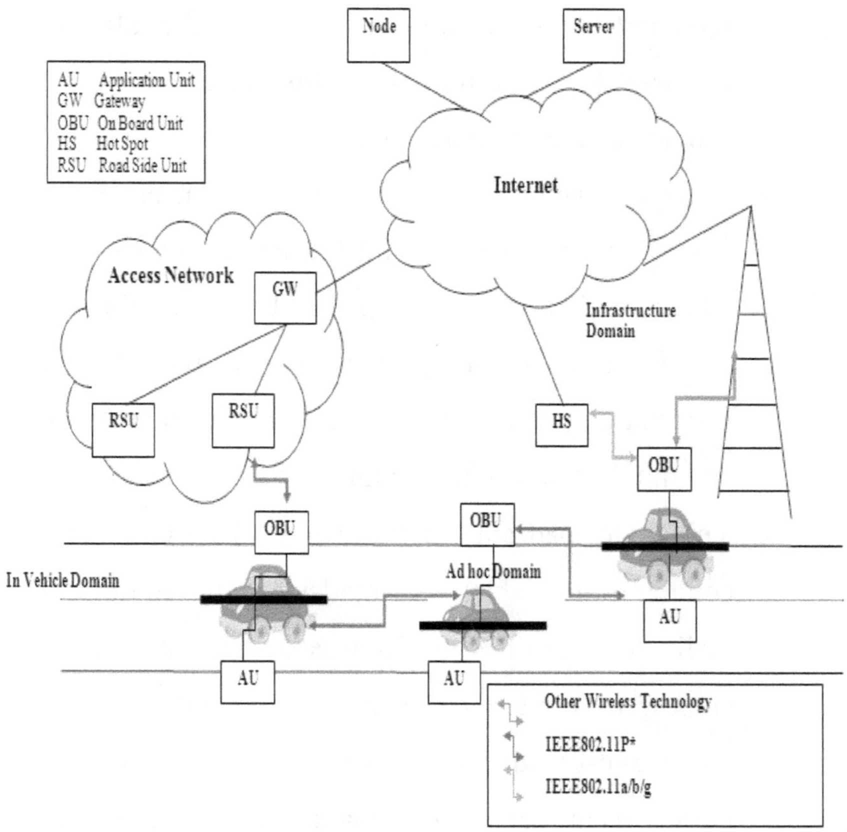

Figure 1.1 C2C-CC Reference Architecture

The in-vehicle domain consists of an on-board unit (OBU) and one or numerous application units (AUs), which are connected either wired or wirelessly (Huang *et al.* 2017). Ad-hoc network is defined as the number of vehicles that are fitted with OBUs and RSUs. In this, OBU functions as a mobile node of MANET while RSU is installed at a place, which is connected to the internet through the Gateway. In infrastructure domain, OBUs can connect with internet through RSUs and hot spots (HSs). In this domain, OBUs can also communicate with one another with the help of cellular radio networks (GSM, GPRS, UMTS, WiMAX, and 4G) with no RSUs and HSs being present.

The communication in VANETs is classified into four kinds i.e. In-Vehicle, V2V, V2I and V2B communication (Hasrouny *et al.* 2017).

- In-vehicle communication is critical for the safety of driver and public. It identifies a vehicle's performance and driver's tiredness and somnolence in in-vehicle domain.
- Vehicle-to-vehicle (V2V) communication enables the communication among vehicles with no infrastructure utilizes in-vehicle equipments, which renders driving help for the driver for sharing messages for warning and alert along with information with one another like lane margining and automated cruise-control application. V2V communication is either single hop or multi-hop.
- Vehicle-to-road side infrastructure (V2I) communication helps in the communication between roadside unit equipment and vehicles to facilitate real-time traffic/weather updates for drivers and also empowers with environmental sensing and monitoring.
- Vehicle-to-broadband cloud (V2B) communication consists of infotainment, data monitoring and traffic information with the help of 3G/4G wireless broadband mechanism. This kind of communication is helpful for providing driving assistance and vehicle tracking.

1.2 CHARACTERISTICS OF VANET

Even though VANET is a subcategory of MANET, but offers its own unique features. The properties of VANET are the following (Hamdi *et al.* 2020):

Highly dynamic network topology: Owing to the high mobility of vehicles on various available path selections results in network changes often.

Predictable Mobility: In comparison with MANET, the movement of vehicles is limited by road topology, and navigation by road maps may be really useful in the prediction of the position and location of vehicles on roads.

No Power limitations: The power backup to the OBU is constantly provided by the battery available in the vehicles resulting in zero power limits.

Fast computational ability: Vehicles are fitted with different computational resources (like processors, excessive memory power, global positioning systems (GPS), and antenna) and sensors which help in efficient wireless communication among vehicles and also to get the vehicle's present position, speed and direction led to increase in computational capability of vehicle.

Unbounded network size: Since VANET can strongly connect one or more number of cities or even a nation, VANET exhibits scalability for an infinite size of its network.

1.3 APPLICATIONS AND TECHNICAL ISSUES IN VANET

The applications of vehicular communication are categorized into 5 groups, which are shown in Figure 1.2 and is explained as follows (Lee & Atkison 2020). These are not the full applications, though still they represent the much broader segment of VANET research.

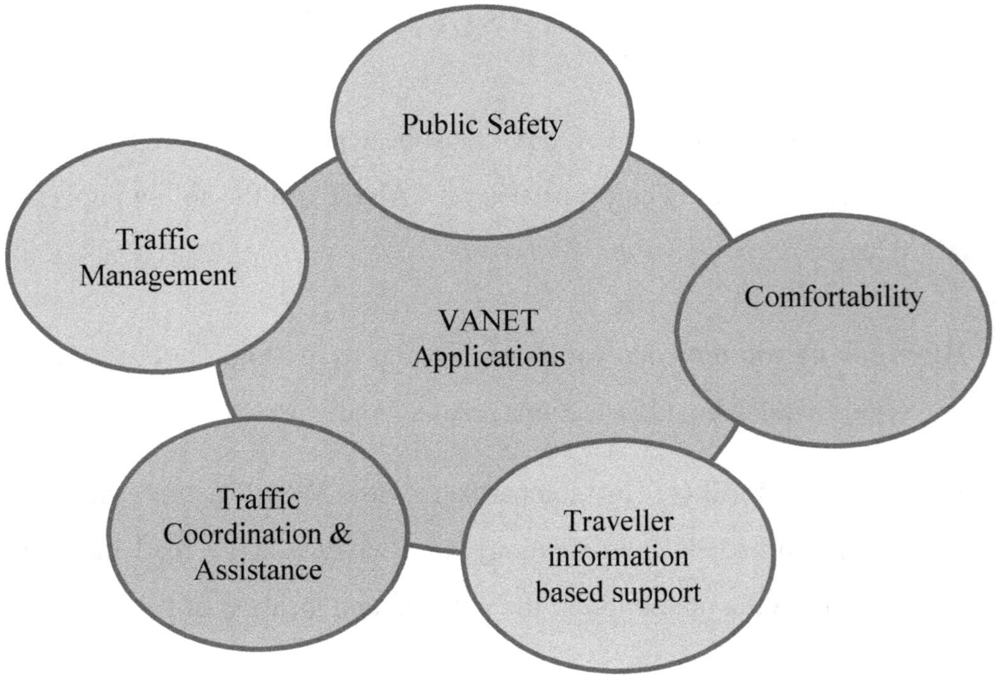

Figure 1.2 VANET applications

Public Safety: It is one of the critical concerns in vehicular communication system. Public safety application concentrates on averting accidents and avoids the loss of drivers' life and also that of the passengers of vehicles. It consists of post-crash alerts, road hazard control notification, suitable curve and road speed warning, collision warning, road condition, present weather situation, emergency breaking, collaborative collision warning, and intersection collision warning etc.

Traffic Management: It is connected with the traffic flow management in such a manner that it prevents accidents, congestions and travel time. The traffic management applications include real-time traffic prediction monitoring, traffic lights scheduling, emergency vehicle awareness, and selection of routes during congestion etc.

Traffic Coordination and assistance: It is one of the important research fields of V2V communication. It includes lane changing help, platooning, which can improve the traffic handling in roads and available highways.

Traveler information support: It is involved with revealing traffic information needed to the traveler when travelling. Its applications consist of local updated maps, location of neighborhood parking slots, gas stations and public places such as museum, park etc. It also includes road warning information.

Comfort-ability: It is about with the comfort of both the driver and passengers so that the ride can be more pleasant when using their spare time in accessing internet like web services (email, audio-video sharing, web browsing, file sharing etc.), online parking payment, toll collection etc.

1.3.1 Challenges

The primary technical problems encountered by vehicular network are explained as follows (Hasrouny *et al.* 2017):

Connectivity: Owing to higher mobility and dynamic network topology, there are quick network divisions and need time and high transmission power, which further deteriorate the throughput. Hence, it is one among the primary problems of VANET, which has gained the attention of the researchers and automotive field.

Signal fading: Owing to the existence of buildings, trees and intermediate vehicles moving between two communicating vehicles results the attenuation of signal before getting to their intended vehicle. Therefore, it has a huge effect on the efficacy of vehicular communication.

Bandwidth limitations: Bandwidth is a scarce resource. Since no centralized control exists among vehicles and road side units, bandwidth management and contention operation is immediately required. In hugely dense environment, a larger probability of channel congestion resulting in a very less bandwidth range (10-20MHz) is seen.

Routing Protocol: Development of an effective routing protocol is one of the critical tasks in developing VANET. A useful routing protocol improves the packet delivery ratio, yields the shortest and best routes to be selected during the time of congestion, limits the interferences resulting due to buildings and tress, and prevents obstructions and congestions.

Security and Privacy: Security and privacy hogs a huge deal of focus of the VANET research group. It involves the authenticity of the vehicle present in communication, different attacks and false data moving around during communication.

1.4 INTELLIGENT TRANSPORTATION SYSTEM

Repetitive traffic jams happening daily are a depiction of the fact that the road networks are not capable of coping up with the demand for mobility that will still see an increase in the future to come (Lin *et al.* 2017). Particularly, in densely populated areas, such as the state of North Rhine-Westphalia, it is socially unreasonable to extend the road network more for mitigating the condition. In addition, construction of new roadway capacities is hugely cumbersome. Therefore, one of the goals of Intelligent Transportation System (ITS) is emphasize more on the efficient usage of the available infrastructure, e.g., by rendering information to the road users. Analysis on driver information technologies has evolved by the 1950s and has developed in the last 50 years. Even though the technologies have progressed, the main objectives are the same:

- boost the travel efficiency and mobility
- improve safety
- provide economic advantages
- preserve energy

• safeguard the environment

In the recent times, the progress of modern technologies in information processing, sensing, and computer control, e.g., Global Positioning Systems (GPS) or the Internet, have fostered the development of ITS. This will have a significant impact in the field of transportation in many countries.

1.4.1 ITS Areas

Generally, ITS applications have been sub classified into six interconnected technology fields (Rahim 2017):

Advanced Traveller Management Systems (ATMS): ATMS monitor, control, and management of traffic on roads and freeways to decrease the congestion and increase the efficiency utilizing vehicle route diversion, automated signal timing, Variable Message Signs (VMS), and priority control systems.

Advanced Traveller Information Systems (ATIS): ATIS consists of several systems, which render real-time, in-vehicle information to drivers with respect to navigation and route direction, motorist services, roadway signings, and hazard alerts.

Advanced Vehicle Control Systems (AVCS): AVCS generally highlight on in-car usage and indicate systems, which help the drivers to control their vehicle, especially during emergency conditions and eventually getting a hold on few or all driving tasks. Instances include Automatic Cruise Control (ACC) systems, which bring up emergency braking when the distance to the predecessor goes below the threshold.

Commercial Vehicle Operations (CVO): CVO introduces the application of ITS technologies for the specific requirements of commercial vehicles, which includes automated vehicle identification, location, weigh in-motion, clearance sensing, and record maintenance. One important challenge in this domain is the improvement of fleet management functions.

Advanced Rural Transportation Systems (ARTS): ARTS consists of systems, which use ITS technology for the specific requirements of rural regions, as these are defined by several attributes, which are diverse from urban regions, e.g., blind corners, lesser passing lanes, long-distance travel or less assisting infrastructure.

Advanced Public Transportation Systems (APTS): APTS improves the efficiency, attraction, and efficacy of public transportation and consists of automatic fare collection, public travel security, and particularly real-time information systems. But, this information must help the multi-model part, as the availability and accessibility of information is one of the important disadvantages of public transport. This research work highlights on ATIS and ATMS. The mechanisms of the two techniques are contradictory, as the distribution of control is done in various means. On one side, the management systems attempt attaining a control universally, i.e., for traffic monitoring, analyzing the patterns, and then performing their regulation using signs, or ramp meters. On the other side, ATIS yields information or even suggestions to the road users. However, it is their individual preference to adopt, neglect or just perform the contrary of the suggestions. Only thing common in both systems are that they attempt improving the efficacy of the traffic flow. To collect the necessary information, different detection devices are utilized.

1.4.2 Technologies

There are few innovative technologies, which encourage the progress of ITS, e.g., GPS, GSM, Internet (Eswaraprasad & Raja 2017). The Global Positioning System (GPS) holds significance as it permits finding the location of an object utilized at least three satellites. The Internet provides massive possibilities for the distribution of information. It will be made available on in-vehicle devices in the near future. Recently, several web-pages already provide real-time information on the traffic conditions to the user.

1.4.2.1 Temporal Nature of Information

As the concept of ITS is to render information, the temporal behaviour of the data and also its usage in traffic conditions must be discussed in short (D'Urso *et al.* 2019). By concept, information may be divided into three different temporal classes:

Historical Data: Historical or after-trip information depicts the earlier states of the network. It can be either objective (measured), or subjective (individual experience). The objective historical data are helpful in classifying the everyday traffic demands and extraction of heuristics, which can be utilized for traffic forecasting.

Current Data: The present information is given real-time and must be the updated information to the latest.

Predictive Data: This type of data depicts the anticipated traffic scenarios. The predictive information could be short-duration, up to one hour, or long-duration, up to one day. To render this data, smart algorithms are required to integrate historical and predictive data.

1.4.2.2 Information in Traffic Systems

All the temporal classes of data are given prior to a trip or during the trip (Ding *et al.* 2016):

Pre-Trip Information: The transmission of the data is done over the Internet or GSM. As there is enough time for the road user to analyses and then process it, the amount of information can be massive compared to en-route systems. This type of information presents the everyday dynamics of the route selections behaviour into traffic systems.

En-Route Information: In order to support the road user during his trip data are transmitted enroute or on-trip. Possible modes of transmission are Variable Message Signs (VMS) or radio broadcast. Therefore, the content and amount of information can vary strongly. In general, it should be short and concise. In contrast to pre-trip, en-route information leads to within day-dynamics of the route choice behaviour.

1.5 ROUTING IN VANET

Owing to highest mobility, topology changes happening frequently and less lifespan are such features of this network making the routing decisions to be a huge challenge (Purkait & Tripathi 2020). Various other factors including road layout and diverse environments like city and highway increase the challenges faced by routing in VANET. In contrary to topology based routing of MANET, VANET utilizes the position information of the member nodes within the network to make routing decisions.

1.5.1 Routing Protocols in VANET

The high mobility characteristic of VANET makes the usage of the right routing protocol to be a huge challenge (Devangavi & Gupta 2017). The packets in the network are transmitted between vehicles, which are moving with high speed and in addition there is also an increase and decrease in the density of vehicles that leads to a rise in the challenges associated with routing protocols. Owing to the huge problematic nature of VANET, the researcher have developed various kinds of protocols that will be described in sections that follow. Also, Figure 1.3 illustrates the classification of routing protocols.

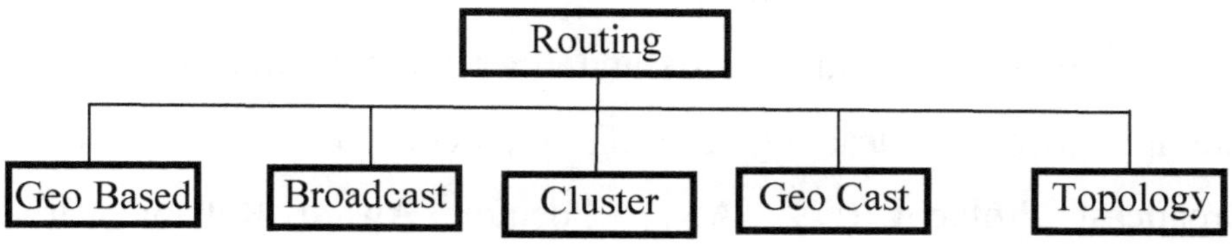

Figure 1.3 Classification Routing Protocols

1.5.1.1 Geo based Protocols

In this kind of protocol, a source will use the geographical positions and also the network address to communicate with the destination (Patel *et al.* 2016). Load Balancing Routing Protocol (LBRP) computes and also configures the route according to the information on the basis of the position of nodes. Hence, the routing tables are not required to be built. The protocol includes three components like beaconing, location and forwarding services. The disadvantage of this protocol is that it needs the help of Global Positioning System (GPS) to obtain the location of the vehicle. Also, the strength of the satellite signals reduces once the vehicle gets into the area such as tunnel. However, as to the highway environment is considered, the best performance is achieved. Also, its benefits include efficiency in high mobile environment. Instances of these protocols include Greedy Perimeter Stateless Routing (GPSR) and Distance Routing Effect Algorithm for Mobility (DREAM).

1.5.1.2 Broadcast based Routing Protocols

This protocol inundates the data packet to the whole VANET and every available node present in the propagation domain (Stajkic *et al.* 2020). The mentioned protocol is utilized each and every time the destination node goes out of the range of transmission of the source node. Generally, these protocols are employed with application, which are bothered about the safety of road, weather condition alerts and emergency warning messages etc. Few examples of broadcasting routing protocols are Distributed Vehicular Broadcast Protocol (DV-CAST), Position Aware Reliable Broadcasting Protocol (POCA) and Density Aware Reliable Broadcasting Protocol (DECA). The valid point of the mentioned protocols is its robustness. However, the bandwidth consumption of these kinds of protocols is high and several duplicate packets reach the node that, in turn, is not beneficial for the performance of protocol.

1.5.1.3 Cluster based Routing Protocols

In this protocol, the vehicle having same features like the speed, direction etc. are integrated in one cluster (Abuashour & Kadoch 2017). Also, in case a vehicle node has to communicate with the node present within the cluster, then the data will use a direct path since it is taken as a local communication. In case the vehicle node requires communication with the node that is external to the cluster, then it needs the support of its cluster head for getting to the destination. The scalability aspects renders it a good preference for the network designers. However, traffic delays is its disadvantages. Clustering for Open Inter vehicular communication Network (COIN) is the main example of this protocol.

1.5.1.4 Geo cast Routing Protocols

Geo cast protocol comprises of two important zones, which are Zone Of Relevance (ZOR) and Zone Of Forwarding (ZOF). ZOR is that region devoted for the nodes of that area. The primary objective of this protocol is to get communication happen between the vehicle existing in ZOR. Also, in case the source vehicle desires to communicate with the vehicle not present in ZOR of that vehicle then that vehicle will become a member of ZOF and any vehicle coming in ZOF is responsible for forwarding the information to other ZORs. Owing to the changes happening frequently in the zones, the connection and disconnection can occur constantly.

1.5.1.5 Topology based Routing Protocols

This section highlights on topology based protocols (Salman *et al.* 2016). The abovementioned type includes two types of protocol, which include proactive and reactive. Also, Figure 1.4 illustrates the classification of routing protocols employed in ad-hoc environment.

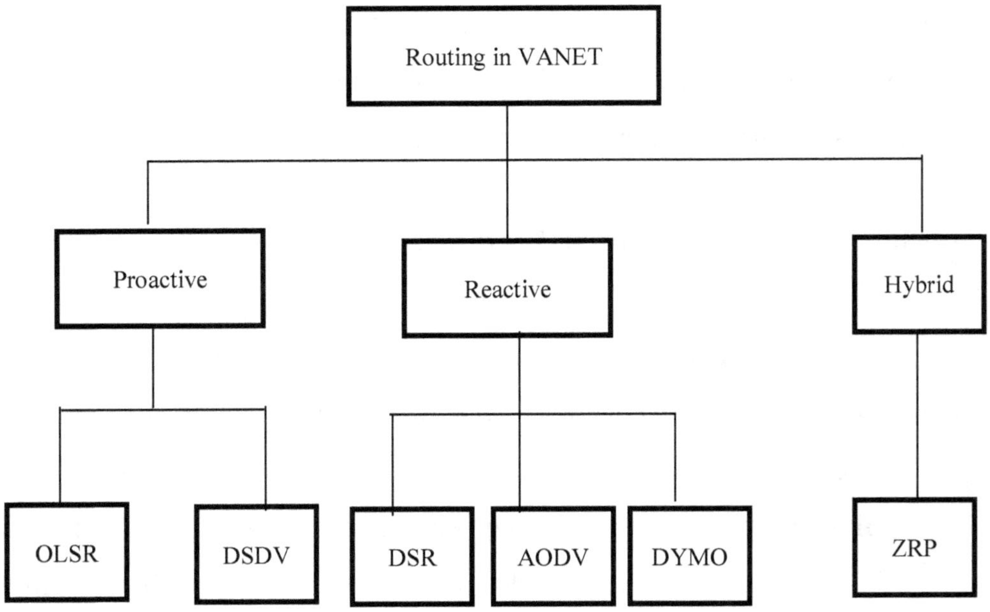

Figure 1.4 Classification of Adhoc Routing Protocols

Proactive Protocols: The protocols continues computing the route periodically and hence, there are frequent changes or updates in the routing table (Setiabudi *et al.* 2016). These protocols utilize Bellman Ford Algorithm in which all the nodes maintain the information associated to the next node. One benefit of the abovementioned protocol is that the route will publish each and every time a packet desires to transmit a data. Example of these protocol consists of Optimized Link State Routing (OLSR) and Destination Sequenced Distance Vector (DSDV) protocol. OLSR is just a fine-tuned variant of link state protocol. The operation of link state protocol is such that any modification in a topology will be propagates to every node in a network that will make the network overhead increase. OLSR deal with two types of messages such hello and a message for managing the topology. Hello messages are utilized to get the data on the connection status. Multi Point Relay (MPR) is chosen when topology control message is utilized for broadcasting its own neighbor information. By using MPR, the overload has decreased like in pure link state protocol. DSDV protocol is a modified form of Bellman Ford Algorithm. This algorithm helped resolve the issue of looping in routing by saving the sequence number information of every node.

Reactive Protocols: This type of protocols does not have the information on every node (Chbib *et al.* 2020). It only maintains the information of the nodes coming into the route. The examples of reactive protocols include an Ad-hoc On-Demand Distance Vector (AODV), Dynamic Source Control Routing (DSR) and Dynamic Manet on Demand (DYMO) protocol. AODV is the most popular protocol in VANET. It has the information on next hop for the destination nodes. In addition, every routing table is maintained for a particular time. In case, a route is not demanded within the particular time then the route expiry will happen and a new route will be specified on demand. According to AODV, each and every time a source node desires to transmit a data to the destination node, it will verify the route in its routing table. In case the route information is present in the table, then the packet will be relayed to the destination. Else, the source node will propagate the route discovery request to the neighbours. AODV is a mobile ad-hoc protocol desirable in a highly crowded traffic. The abovementioned protocols have helped to decrease the broadcasting overhead. Also, route discovery process will be carried out on demand. DSR is an efficient protocol used for routing. It is fundamentally created for multi-hop Wireless Adhoc NETwork (WANET). It is a self-arranging and configuring protocol, which does not need any management. The two important functions of the mentioned protocol include route discovery and maintenance. The mentioned functions operate with one another for node discovery and route maintenance. DYMO is one more on demand protocol developed after AODV. DYMO routing protocol can be realized to be proactive and also reactive. In addition, route discovery strategy is on demand each and every time needed.

Hybrid Protocols: Hybrid is a mixture of proactive and reactive routing protocols that helps decrease the overhead and helps delaying occurrence owing to the regular sharing of topology information. Using the hybrid mechanism, the productivity and scalability feature of network has increased. Meanwhile, the disadvantage of hybrid mechanism is its high delay while moving through new routes. The popular protocol that depends on hybrid scheme is Zone Routing Protocol (ZRP).

1.6 ROUTING CHALLENGES IN VANET

Therefore, it is necessary to develop routing protocol, which considers the problems and features of the vehicular network. Few technical issues and design alternates are listed as below (Ahamed & Vakilzadian 2018):

1) Scalability: Scalability is one of the important features of VANETs. Therefore, the performance of the routing protocol should exhibit reduced effect on different number of vehicles in the network. This is attainable when the protocol has the ability of carrying out localized operations where the routing decisions made by a node are only dependent on information present in its neighbourhood. This averts the requirement for the node to be aware of the topology of the whole network, thus limiting the control overhead.

2) Neighbourhood Discovery: One of the basic functions of the routing protocol is neighbourhood discovery, which can be carried out either during route establishment process or by transmitting one hop control messages known as beacons. Usage of small periodic interval for beaconing may result in increased control overhead, while large periodic interval for beaconing indicates old neighbourhood information. Therefore, selecting the periodic interval right for beaconing is necessary for achieving a better balance between trade-off between control overhead and updated information. Few approaches utilize adaptive beaconing depending on particular features of the vehicular environment including mobility and density. Few authors have authored elaborate survey on different beaconing approaches in VANET by focusing on their performance needs, key characteristics and future directions. One more updated and more popular scheme is the beaconless mechanism, which includes the reactive discovery of neighbours while data packets are forwarded.

3) Data Forwarding: Classical ad-hoc routing protocols have routing tables, which include information about the next hop for reaching the destination depending on particular conditions. Even though these types of routing protocols have been realized in VANETs, they lead to deteriorated performance, particularly in extremely dynamic environments. A probable solution to this is to perform the data routing based on per hop, where a forwarding node routes the data packet as per its neighbourhood at the right time of the message forwarding.

4) Uneven Vehicle Density: The vehicular environment also experience problems with irregular vehicle density, where few regions may face sparse traffic environment whereas others may be crowded. The routing protocol must adapt to the changing traffic density scenarios. If there is heavy congestion in the region, the protocol should have the ability of discovering a path providing reduced congestion. In less traffic scenarios, a vehicle can save the message till there is a chance for desirable forwarding. Also, it would be favourable to include an adaptive approach, which modifies its mode of operation depending on the traffic scenario.

5) Use of Positional Information: Vehicles in VANET can access positional information using navigational tools like GPS. This information can provide important benefits to routing solutions. It is much recommended for routing protocols to consider the positional information when choosing path and neighbours since these will further help in improving the routing performance.

6) Prediction of Future Positions: The limited mobility pattern and the availability to positional information permit's a vehicle in the prediction of positions in the future. This information can help the protocol to take routing decisions with efficiency. But, caution must be undertaken in the prediction process since inexact information may result in choosing a non-optimal path.

1.7 NEED OF FUEL CONSUMPTION IN VANET

Recently, the problem of energy saving is gaining much popularity in ITS. The current rise in fuel cost hugely influences the economic changes happening globally. The drivers are bogged down about their fuel usage fitting their monthly budget. Unrestrained usage of petroleum not just makes the budget increase but also leads to more pollutants being discharged. The Texas A&M Transportation Institute has observed that owing to congestion, urban Americans need to travel 5.5 billion hours more and they are needed to buy an addition 2.9 billion gallons of fuel for a congestion cost of $121 billion whereas 56 billion pounds of more Carbon Monoxide (CO) and greenhouse gas discharged into the atmosphere during urban congested environments just in 2011 (Rehman *et al.* 2018). The world right now is affected badly by environmental pollution. Therefore, reducing the fuel usage can reduce the pollutant discharge and keep the clean and green beauty of the environment. Even though considerably research has been carried out by several researchers in the domain of fuel and energy for alternate fuels, the automotive industry also tried to boost vehicle modernization for fuel productivity and economically feasible environment friendly technology.

ITS can be defined to be wire and wireless communications depending on information and electronics technologies combined with transportation system and vehicles. It is an advanced approach for the green technology, which not just changes a single vehicle to green but also changes the entire bunch of vehicles green. ITS has already stirred a revolution in the domain of transportation systems. ITS includes a broad array of approaches and technologies like real-time traffic information systems (TIS), electronic toll collection system (ETCS), and automated traffic light control system (ATLCS). It is possible to evolve as the primary tool for resolving surface transportation problems over the next few years, since an infrastructure is developed along with physical transportation infrastructure. This system implements communications, control, electronics, and computer technologies to boost the performance of road transportation systems.

ITS technologies are not ambitious or futuristic; they are original, and are already present in various nations now, and are accessible to all countries, which highlight on designing and implementing them (Slonim 2020). ITS is a potential technology, which can be utilized for decreasing the fuel usage and exhaust pollutant that helps save the environment. The technologies mitigate congestion, render innovative safety, and improve efficiency. ITS application is utilized for reducing the average distance, travel time, and traffic density estimation. It can be utilized for green goals by notifying the driver about the best path, which can limit the considerable amount of fuel since the choice of the vehicle is the route having less congestion. Vehicles can send and receive message having vital data and look for best path as per their location, speed, and direction. A smart vehicle gathers data utilizing few special sensors. Once this data is processed, it propagates the information to other vehicles. A huge number of vehicles presently are powered by fossil fuels. Therefore, considerable improvement is needed for ITS to decrease fuel usage and also pollutants which in turn helps avoiding the global warming and greenhouse gas. The ITS technologies encourage the decrease of fuel usage with two factors, first to limit congestion maintaining the optimal speed of every vehicle and secondly to recommend the driver for a green fuel productive path.

1.8 PROBLEM DEFINITION

With the rising development in this rapidly moving society, vehicles have evolved to be the primary requirement compared to a luxury item. Traffic jams have been rising from then. This rise in traffic jams has been in direct proportion to fuel usage resulting in displeasure and irritation to drivers. VANET (Vehicular Ad Hoc Network) is not just effective but also secure comfortable and robust alternates to the recent transportation systems. The important challenges observed in the fuel usage sensitive routing in VANET are given as follows:

- Data communication is not focused in the available work that is important to take rapid decision associated with vehicle control, and this way the fuel usage can be controlled.
- Communication between various SDN agent RSUs existing in multiple layers are hard to compute owing to coverage problems.
- Successful and robust data transmission is not highlighted in this technical work which is needed for an efficient decision making that leads to the necessity of routing strategy to increase.

1.9 OBJECTIVE OF THE RESEARCH

Fuel efficient vehicles need less amount of gas to travel a particular distance. When less gas is burnt, global warming emissions are cut and pollution is reduced, when the expense on gas is less—a way more less. Driving with a steady and smooth hand will help increase fuel efficiency, since abrupt braking, strong accelerating and "revving" your vehicle leads to increase in fuel usage. The best means of driving smoothly is to be alert and be sensitive of the roads every time. Therefore, it is essential to analyze the effect of VANET communication on the performance of transportation applications. This effect depends on the ITS application also and its sensitivity to the completeness, correctness, and the spatial distribution of the data. One of these applications includes feedback-based eco-routing (FB-ECO) navigation. The primary goal of this technical work is to realize the model which can result in productive routing in the VANET environment with decreased fuel depletion and delay.

1.10 MOTIVATION OF THE RESEARCH

The reasons for inspiring this research are briefly explained in this section. Universally, fuel productivity of vehicles is attaining centralized focus within the aspects of climate changes, public health, and decreasing the dependency on oil. In India, earnest efforts have been made to devise fuel efficiency standards for vehicles. The vehicular fleet in Indian cities is much younger compared to the affluent countries of the European Union and in the US, where the average age of cars is 8 years and 11 years, correspondingly. The extreme social and economical effects of fuel usage have influenced the research towards Vehicular Ad-hoc Networks (VANETs). VANETs will improve driver safety and minimize the traffic and fuel depletion by realizing collision prevention and warning systems.

1.11 RESEARCH CONTRIBUTION

The important contribution made by this technical work is listed as below:

- Presenting Re-Grouping approach to limit the fuel depletion and CO_2 discharge in the VANET environment

- ➢ Realizing the fuel usage and delay sensitive traffic scheduling approach for optimized VANET routing
- ➢ Presenting Dynamic VANET routing approach for decreasing the fuel usage with the problem of coverage challenges in VANET environment

1.12 ORGANIZATION OF THE THESIS

The research work is organized as below:

This chapter gives an elaborate introduction on the vehicular adhoc network and its features. This chapter also studies the various routing approaches and different routing protocols realized for the VANET environment. This chapter also analyzes the necessity for fuel usage in the VANET environment and the problems faced have been studied. This chapter also discusses about the problem definition, goals and inspiration of the overall research work.

Chapter 2 discusses about the various associated research approaches. This chapter gives the elaborate analysis of the various research approaches, presented by multiple authors towards the fuel consumption sensitive routing in the VANET environment. This chapter also elaborately review the advantages and drawbacks of different research approaches.

Chapter 3 discusses the overview and elaborate analysis on the Regrouping technique based fuel consumption reduced routing. This chapter gives the appropriate example and diagrams for the proposed research approach called as regrouping technique.

Chapter 4 provides the extensive overview on the discussed research approach called as fuel depletion and delay sensitive traffic scheduling along with appropriate examples and necessary diagrams. This section also reviews the numerical analysis performed with the needed description.

Chapter 5 discusses the coverage and load aware routing in the VANET environment in detail. This work explains about the important objective of the research work with appropriate examples and explanation.

Chapter 6 explains about the analysis carried out on the proposed and the available research approaches on the basis of the simulation results achieved.

Chapter 7 provides the conclusion of the research work along with research works intended to be performed in the future.

1.13 SUMMARY

In this chapter, detailed introduction about the vehicular adhoc network and their characteristics is given. This chapter also provides the detailed overview of the intelligent transport system and the role of routing protocols. And also this chapter provides the overall view about the need of fuel consumption in VANET and the routing protocols that attempt to attain the fuel consumption is given. Finally this chapter concluded with the problem definition and the objective and motivation of the research work along with overall research contribution.

CHAPTER 2

LITERATURE REVIEW

2.1 FUEL CONSUMPTION IN VANET

Rehman *et al.* (2018) presented Vehicular Ad-hoc Network (VANET) based routing algorithm for SPS known as Updating Block Route Algorithm (UBRA). It functions by identifying congestion and by computing the average speed of the vehicles. The discussed UBRA helps updating the route with less congested route and its installation expenditure is less. Also, it provides reduced parking area search time, fuel usage and carbon dioxide (CO_2) discharge.

Elbery & Rakha (2018) presented a novel scalable architecture for communication modeling in vehicular networks. This model facilitates the mutual effect and interaction happening in the communication and transportation system to be analysed. One significant benefit of the discussed model is its scalability, which provides support to tens of thousands of parallel vehicles in the network. This model is designed and utilized for evaluating the effect of communication on the performance of a dynamic eco-routing application.

Doolan & Muntean (2016) introduced EcoTrec, a vehicular ad hoc network-based vehicle routing solution developed to decrease the vehicle carbon discharge with no considerable effect on the travel times of vehicles.

The vehicles interchange messages associated with traffic and road conditions, like average speed on the road, road gradient, and surface condition. This information is utilized for building a fuel efficiency model of the routes, depending on which the vehicles are suggested to use routes that are more efficient. By routing the vehicles more productively, with the reduction of the greenhouse emissions and less degrees of traffic congestion.

Chou *et al.* (2017) used the vehicular ad hoc networks (VANETs) technology to construct a virtual traffic light (VTL) environment to minimize the traffic congestion. The aim of this work is to modify the length of the traffic light signal time on-demand to facilitate the vehicles to go through several intersections quickly, thus preserving energy and decreasing the fuel depletion. The traffic phase combination algorithm and VTL operation techniques are also studied to cope up with the traffic congestion conditions in urban regions.

Bhargava *et al.* (2017) used the principle of weighted variables and Dijkstra's for predicting the most practical path having the lowest traffic density and congestion. But, this system is susceptible to different active and passive attacks, and hence, to tackle with the problem of secured transmission of information between the OBU's and the cloud, a security strategy is defined, where the Certification Authority (CA) would be the centre, accountable for enrolling vehicles, supervising loyalty and distributing keys. This security framework utilizes pre-available algorithms such RSA and Hashing to get favourable results.

Khatri *et al.* (2020) evaluated different machine learning algorithms for the VANET based traffic control. These algorithms render effective supervised and unsupervised learning of these gathered data, which helps in productively implementing the aim of VANET. The safety, communication, and traffic-associated problems in VANET systems is studied and the feasibility of its implementation is analyzed and the way in which machine learning algorithms can get over these problems are explored. At last, the future direction and problems are discussed, in addition to a case study showing a VANET based environment.

Campolina *et al.* (2018) showed how Deep Neural Networks is applied to vehicular sensor data. The first objective of this research work is to generate man-made readings for two sensors having missing values, which include CO_2 and fuel consumption. A neural network was trained for generating these values, and it has the capability of getting the approximate function of these two sensors, even though small changes are possible. For training a Multilayer Perceptron (MLP), data from the enviroCar project is used, which aggregates the sensor readings from participants worldwide. Using the dataset having the values produced by the MLP, the impact of these inferences in tracing routes concentrated on fuel efficacy over a graph depending on the traffic network of Monchengladbach.

Saini & Singh (2018) recommended a new congestion minimization approach that highlights on fine-tuning an available congestion minimization technique, which carries out routing employing an optimal relaying distance function and faces high packet losses. The discussed congestion minimization algorithm uses social associations among the nodes to perform the next hop selection employing dynamic optimization with BFO so that packet delivery probability is increased and increased packet delivery rates be attained. The simulation of the discussed approach is done with the help of ONE simulator and its performance is assessed in terms of parameters including Throughput, Packet Drops, Latency and Overhead Ratio.

Zhang *et al.* (2019) introduced a new information perturbation technique, in contrary to the base of autonomously obstructing the data in every broadcast. Particularly, the technique is used for the transmitted vehicle speed, and this corrupted data is utilized in an optimal speed planner to develop a fuel and emissions effective speed path. The results indicate a degraded controller performance if privacy is considered under the baseline technique.

Bousbaa *et al.* (2018) recommended a Time-Limited Reliable Broadcast Incremental Power (TRBIP) algorithm, a central heuristic to limit the transmission disruptions for safety message distribution in VANETs. By limiting the overall transmission energy and the number of hops, TRBIP is capable of reducing the transmission interruption and this way, increases the reliability. Also, in TRBIP, VANETs' features including vehicle mobility and frequent network division are also considered using store-carry-and-forward and the periodic multicast tree reconstruction mechanisms. But, multicast tree management is difficult to maintain in urban regions owing to the high density of nodes in VANETs (big trees), and is impacted by the city streets organizations. In the below Table 2.1 comparison analysis is given.

Table 2.1 Comparison analysis of fuel consumption in VANET

S.No	Author	Method	Merits	Demerits
1	Rehman *et al.* (2018)	Updating Block Route Algorithm	Low installation cost Congestion less route	More computation time
2	Elbery & Rakha (2018)	New scalable framework	Increased fuel consumption efficiency	Increased computation overhead
3	Doolan & Muntean (2016)	EcoTrec	More computation efficiency	Higher processing complexity

			Low traffic congestion levels	Increased vehicles leads to increased congestion
4	Chou *et al.* (2017)	virtual traffic light (VTL) environment	Average speed Increased traffic flow	Higher energy consumption
5	Bhargava *et al.* (2017)	weighted variables and Dijkstra's	Best possible path detection	Increased interference rate
6	Khatri *et al.* (2020)	Machine learning algorithms	Better handling of traffic related issues Ensured safety levels	More routing overhead
7	Campolina *et al.* (2018)	Deep Neural Networks	Better fuel consumption rate Better ECO handling	Increased traffic rate would leads to increased congestion rate
8	Saini & Singh (2017)	congestion minimization technique	Increased throughput Reduced latency	More energy consumption
9	Zhang *et al.* (2019)	novel information perturbation mechanism	Improved controller performance	More computation overhead
10	Bousbaa *et al.* (2018)	Time-Limited Reliable Broadcast Incremental Power (TRBIP) algorithm	Reduced average delay Increased packet delivery ratio	More overhead

2.2 VANET ROUTING PROTOCOLS

Ali *et al.* (2016) comprehensively evaluated three popular MANET routing protocols, AODV, OLSR and GPSR, found in VANET in urban setup. Their performance is compared in terms of three metrics, like Drop Burst Length (DEL) delay and Packet Delivery Ratio (PDR). The simulations are conducted employing NS2 and SUMO simulators platforms, with scenarios setup to mirror the real-world scenarios. The results indicate that OLSR has the capability of attaining a shorter DEL and shows better PDR performance in comparison with AODV and GPSR under less network load.

Lin *et al.* (2016) developed a moving-zone based infrastructure in which vehicles coordinate with each other to create dynamic moving zones so that information distribution is facilitated. Authors introduced a new scheme, which presents shifting object modelling and indexing approaches from the theory of big moving object databases into the design of VANET routing protocols. The results of elaborate simulation studies performed on real road maps show that this technique outperforms both clustering and non-clustering based routing protocols.

Ji *et al.* (2016) suggested a novel SDN-based geographic routing (SDGR) protocol for VANET, which depends on node location, vehicles density and digital map. Software-Defined Networking (SDN) is utilized for decoupling the network management from data transferring. In SDGR, the central controller collects information of vehicles and yields a global perspective for computing the optimal routing paths.

Boussoufa-Lahlah *et al.* (2018) introduced benchmarked routing protocols that depends on the geographic location of the vehicles. Authors explains the advantages and the drawbacks of these protocols by investigating the inspirations behind designing such protocols and authors specified few probable directions for future research associated with using this category of protocols.

Goel *et al.* (2016) introduced an acute position based routing protocol (APR) for vehicular ad hoc networks (VANETs), whose performance is better if there is an increase in the number of vehicle on the road in comparison with GPSR. Here, it is the assumption of the authors that all vehicles have the knowledge of their own position and include Global Positioning System (GPS). This protocol utilized limited greedy for transferring a data packet and for the recovery process, carry and forwarding mechanism will utilized. Both the vehicle-to-vehicle (V2V) and vehicle to-infrastructure (V2I) communication are used. Every intersection point on the road contain a RSU (Road Side Unit) that makes all the decisions about the path of flow of the data packet. In case, no suitable path exists, then the RSUs will save the data packet till they get the suitable path for transferring the data packet.

Houmer & Hasnaoui (2019) found the effect of different mobility models on the performance of Ad-hoc On-demand Distance Vector (AODV), Cluster-Based Directional Routing (CBDR) and Greedy Perimeter Stateless Routing (GPSR) protocols. In this analysis, the performance of these routing protocols are evaluated in various mobility models such as: Street Random Waypoint (STRWP), Gauss Markov and Freeway exhibiting different speeds.

Abuashour & Kadoch (2017) introduced a new Intersection Dynamic VANET Routing (IDVR) protocol, whose objective is to improve the route stability, average throughput, and minimize the end-to-end delay in a grid topology. Authors have applied a centralized Software Defined Network (SDN) to collect traffic information in real-time and render the Intersection Cluster Head (ICH) a Set of Candidate Shortest Routes (SCSR). At the

Intersection, An ICH algorithm is introduced on the basis of the maximum Life Time (LT), the LT refers to the time that every vehicle needs till it detaches from the cluster. The IDVR protocol chooses the optimal route on the basis of its present location, destination location, and the maximum of the minimum average throughput among the SCSR.

Goudarzi *et al.* (2018) introduced a traffic-sensitive position-based routing protocol for vehicular ad hoc networks (VANETs) desirable for city areas. The protocol is an improved variant of the geographical source routing (GSR) protocol. The discussed protocol, called as effective GSR, utilizes an ant-based algorithm to discover a route having the optimum network connectivity. It is presumed that each vehicle includes a digital map of the streets, which includes junctions and street sections. Making use of information present in small control packets known as ants, the vehicles compute a weight for each street segment in proportion to the network connectivity of that section. Ant packets are propelled by the vehicles in junction regions. To get the optimum route between a source and a destination, the source vehicle decides the path on a street map having the minimum overall weight for the entire route

Haider *et al.* (2019) brought forward using the movement direction and relative locations of source and destination nodes to suit the dynamic bi-directional highway environments for effective and reliable routing of warning messages. A new routing protocol, known as, Direction Aware Best Forwarder Selection (DABFS), is introduced in this work. DABFS considers the directions and relative locations of nodes, in addition to the distance parameter, to decide the node's movement direction employing Hamming distance and then forwards warning messages using neighbour and best route discovery.

Joshua & Varadarajan (2019) discussed about a framework that is based on using network resources to further show the present system condition and modify the setup between constant changes in the network topology and the QoS requirements. It includes three phases: The VANET scenario generator for generating the network road and traffic scenarios, devising the weighted cost function, and at last, the optimization stage to find the optimized configuration depending on the weighted cost function derived. The simulation of the proposed scheme (FA-OLSR) was done and the simulation results showed increase in Packet Delivery Ratio, Mean Routing Load, and End-to-End Delay. In Table 2.2 comparison analysis of VANET routing protocol is shown.

Table 2.2 Comparison analysis of VANET routing protocols

S.No	Author	Method	Merits	Demerits
1	Ali *et al.* (2016)	Analysis of routing protocols	Stable Packet delivery ratio	Increased delay
2	Lin *et al.* (2016)	moving-zone based architecture	Reduced communication overhead Improved message delivery rate	Fuel consumption is not focused
3	Ji *et al.* (2016)	SDN-based geographic routing (SDGR) protocol	Increased packet delivery ratio Reduced delivery delay time	Eco factors are not considered
4	Boussoufa-Lahlah *et al.* (2018)	Analysis of geographic routing protocols	Increased robust Adaptive to increased topology changes	Reduced packet delivery ratio

S.No	Author	Method	Merits	Demerits
5	Goel *et al.* (2016)	Acute position based routing protocol (APR)	Increased packet delivery ratio Decreased delay	Increased traffic rate leads to more congestion rate
6	Houmer & Hasnaoui (2019)	Analysis of impact on different mobility models	Increased packet delivery ratio Increased throughput	More routing delay
7	Abuashour & Kadoch (2017)	Intersection Dynamic VANET Routing (IDVR) protocol	Increased packet delivery ratio Attained minimum average throughput	More energy consumption
8	Goudarzi *et al.* (2018)	Traffic aware VANET routing	More packet delivery ratio Reduced delay	More routing overhead
9	Haider *et al.* (2019)	Direction Aware Best Forwarder Selection (DABFS)	Improved throughput Reduced packet loss rate	Higher routing overhead
10	Joshua & Varadarajan (2019)	Firefly optimization framework	Increased packet delivery ratio	More routing overhead

2.3 DELAY AWARE ROUTING PROTOCOLS IN VANET

Bhover *et al.* (2017) suggested an alternate to help V2X communication rather than the application of WAVE/DSRC. Authors utilized a scalable combination of cellular network, wifi and ZigBee, to balance cellular traffic and mitigate the extra cost, Wi-Fi Direct is utilized in the form of a complementary technique to facilitate communication employing local links with no infrastructure. Zigbee is utilized for connecting road side sensors. The discussed system yields connectivity and monitoring vehicles using a cellular network and using wifi, local data transmission is achieved.

Oliveira *et al.* (2017) introduced a new protocol, Adaptive Data Dissemination Protocol (AddP), whose objective is to render robustness to message distribution efficiently. The protocol utilizes various techniques for the dynamic adjustment of the beacon frequency and to decrease the number of messages and beacons in the network. The efficiency of the discussed protocol and the effects of a VANET safety application using the protocol were assessed carrying out experiments over network and traffic simulators.

Sospeter *et al.* (2019) pioneered an efficient and resourceful adaptive probability data dissemination protocol (EEAPD). EEAPD includes a delay approach and probabilistic scheme. The redundancy ratio (r) metric is considered for describing the relationship between road sections and density of vehicles in rebroadcast probability decisions. The distinct nature of the EEAPD protocol is about considering the number of road segments to determine the nodes that are favourable for the rebroadcast of the emergency message. The final road section is taken into consideration in the transmission range due to its probability of having smaller vehicle density.

Tang *et al.* (2019) recommended centralized routing approach with mobility prediction (CRS-MP) for VANET supported by an artificial intelligence-powered software-defined network (SDN) controller. Particularly, the SDN controller can provide mobility prediction with better accuracy using advanced artificial neural network (ANN) approach. Later, on the basis of the mobility prediction, the estimation of the successful transmission probability and average delay of every vehicle's request under network topology changes happening often can be done with the help of the roadside units (RSUs) or the base station (BS). The estimation is carried out on the basis of a random urban traffic model in which the vehicle arrival adopts a non-homogeneous Poisson process (NHPP). The SDN controller collects the network information from RSUs and BS that are regarded as the switches. Depending on the global network information, the SDN controller helps computing the optimum routing paths for switches (i.e., BS and RSU). When the source vehicle and destination vehicle are positioned in the coverage field of the same switch, the next routing decision will be taken by the RSUs or the BS autonomously to reduce the vehicular service delay on the whole.

Muniyandi *et al.* (2020) introduced an estimation that depends on a heuristic scheme designed to avoid weak GPS location data and take only the accurate ones. The discussed routing protocol called as Rectangle-Aided LAR (RALAR) is dependent on a moving rectangular zone adopting the nodes mobility model. In addition, the discussed RALAR protocol was optimized with the help of the Genetic Algorithm (GA) by choosing the most desirable time-out variable. Then the comparison of the results were done with LAR and Kalman-Filter Aided-LAR (KALAR), the most popular protocols in VANET for performance metrics such as Packet Delivery Ratio (PDR), average End-to-End Delay (E2E Delay), routing overhead and average energy consumption.

Chen *et al.* (2019) demonstrated a road weight evaluation (RWE) algorithm to evaluate the road section, the uniqueness of this is that every road segment has a weight assigned, which depends on two constructed delay models by using the real-time link property if connected or past traffic information if it is disconnected. Using the RWE algorithm, the routing path decided can hugely mitigate the risk of local maximum and data congestion. Specifically, in lieu of the massive size of a progressive city, the road map is split into a set of Grid Zones (GZs). Depending on the destination location, the packets can be relayed among various GZs rather than the entire city map to minimize the computation complexity, where the best path having the least delay within every GZ is decided. The backbone link including a set of chosen backbone nodes at intersections and inside road segments, is constructed for forwarding data along the decided path, which can prevent the MAC competitions also.

Mittal *et al.* (2016) formulated an approach to improve the flexibility of the protocol with the topology varying often. As the vehicle/node in VANET is a quick moving element, the route amongst the nodes face failures often. The algorithm defines an alternative route for transmitting the data packet if there is a link breakage. This method improves the flow rate of data packets in the network and reduces the end-to-end delay.

Li & Chigan (2010) introduces an analytical framework for assessing the effect of transmission range on the end-to-end delay in 802.11p-based VANETs. In comparison with the earlier works, this model obtains a short expression of the transmission delay in saturated networks, and gets the service rate of non-saturated networks using the new technique. As far as the best of the knowledge goes, it is the first whole analytical model, which shows the considerable end-to end delay difference between saturation and non-saturation cases.

Lo & Kuo (2017) introduced a traffic-aware routing protocol (TARCO), which takes integrated real-time traffic conditions into consideration for building delivery paths along a vehicular environment. This objective was attained using three techniques, which include cooperative traffic information collection, concise real-time road scoring and scalable data route construction. An accurate overview of the real-time traffic scenarios was acquired from the collaboration between information aggregator agents at junctions and information collectors on road sections. Every road section later

Cont…

had a weight assigned as per the overall view of the traffic scenarios and then updated frequently to depict the traffic changes. At last, the road sections rendering effective and robust data routes were utilized for building a routing path with assured connectivity and a brief delivery delay to the destination.

Ghafoor *et al.* (2014) introduced a new position-based routing protocol anchor-based connectivity-aware routing (ACAR) for vehicular ad hoc networks (VANETs) to guarantee connectivity of routes with more packets successfully delivered. Both buses and cars are regarded to be vehicular nodes running in both clockwise and anticlockwise directions in a city environment. Both the directions are considered for rapid communication. ACAR is a hybrid protocol, which uses both the greedy forwarding scheme and the store-carry-and-forward technique to reduce the packet drop rate based on particular assumptions. The Authors took just vehicle-to-vehicle (V2V) communication into consideration in which both the source and destination nodes are vehicles in movement. In Table 2.3 comparison analysis of delay aware routing protocols was shown.

Table 2.3 Comparison analysis of Delay aware routing protocols

S.No	Author	Method	Merits	Demerits
1	Bhover *et al.* (2017)	V2X Communication protocol	Reduced delay Lesser energy consumption	ECO factors are not considered
2	Oliveira *et al.* (2017)	Adaptive Data Dissemination Protocol (AddP)	Better congestion control handling Low average delay	Higher congestion rate Increased traffic rate leads to higher interference rate
3	Sospeter *et*	Effective and	Low packet	Finding

S.No	Author	Method	Merits	Demerits
	al. (2019)	efficient adaptive probability data dissemination protocol (EEAPD)	drop ratio	forwarder node process requires more processing overhead
4	Tang *et al.* (2019)	centralized routing scheme	Reduced transmission delay	Frequent mobility of nodes would reduce the overall network performance
5	Muniyandi *et al.* (2020)	Rectangle-Aided LAR (RALAR)	Lesser energy consumption Lesser end to end delay	Higher traffic congestion reduce the packet delivery ratio rate
6	Chen *et al.* (2019)	Road weight evaluation (RWE) algorithm	Increased network performance in terms of packet delivery ratio and throughput Minimum delay	Higher computation overhead
7	Mittal *et al.* (2016)	AODV protocol	Reduced end to end delay Higher packet delivery ratio	Increased mobility would affect the actual end to end delay
8	Li & Chigan (2010)	Analytical model	Lesser end to end delay Increased packet arrival rate	More routing overhead
9	Lo & Kuo (2017)	Traffic-aware routing protocol (TARCO)	Higher network performance	Higher communication overhead

S.No	Author	Method	Merits	Demerits
10	Ghafoor *et al.* (2014)	Position-based routing protocol anchor-based connectivity-aware routing (ACAR)	Increased packet delivery ratio Reduced delay	Increased routing overhead

2.4 COVERAGE AWARE ROUTING PROTOCOLS IN VANET

Darwish *et al.* (2018) introduced a robust traffic sensitive routing protocol, which chooses the next-hop on the basis of structure of roads, predicted positions of neighbours and their received signal strength, and the updated nests of the mobility information obtained from neighbours. The results of simulation revealed considerably improved packet delivery ratio and end-to-end delays.

Bhandari *et al.* (2018) suggested a congestion-aware routing protocol (CoAR) that uses choosing an alternate parent to mitigate the network congestion. The discussed scheme utilizes a multi-criteria decision-making scheme to choose the best alternate parent node within the congestion by integrating the multiple routing metrics. Also, the neighborhood index is considered to be the tie-breaking metric utilized for the parent selection procedure if is equal routing score. For deciding the congestion, CoAR uses the adaptive congestion detection scheme that depends on the present queue occupancy and inferences of current and historic traffic trends.

Kalogeiton *et al.* (2019) designed an algorithm to select the suitable directional antenna for unicasting a message, permitting vehicles external to the spreading region of the message to carry out other tasks. Also, every vehicle helps in route discovery for nodes, which store content, if the content is not restored after a particular time duration. Hence, whenever required, path reconfiguration is done to add new vehicles.

Oubbati *et al.* (2017) analyzed the way in which Unmanned Aerial Vehicle (UAVs) working in random mode can collaborate with VANET on the ground to help in the routing process and boost the robustness of the data delivery by filling the communication gap whenever it is feasible. In this research work, the authors introduced UVAR (UAV-Assisted VANETs routing protocol), which boosts the data routing and connectivity of the vehicles on the ground using UAVs. But, UVAR does not completely use UAVs in the sky for data forwarding as it exploits UAVs solely if there is a highly sparse network.

Rashid *et al.* (2020) explained about the routing, which depends on link stability and to improve the coverage field of the cluster to boost the mobility features and the energy efficacy of the VANET. The outlined studies on both the classifications are explained to increase the link stability, energy efficacy, network lifespan, data aggregation, Quality of service, load balancing and multipath. A proper elaborate survey has been carried out for link stability and energy efficient clustering based routing protocols developed between 2012 and 2018. Using the survey, a technical guidance is given to the researchers on the advantages and drawbacks of the previous studies.

Wu *et al.* (2020) presented a new routing protocol for urban VANETs known as RSU-assisted Q-learning-based Traffic-Aware Routing (QTAR). Integrating the benefits of geographic routing with the static road map information, QTAR is used for learning the road segment traffic information on the basis of the Q-learning algorithm. In QTAR, a routing path comprising of several dynamically chosen high reliability connection road sections, which facilitate packets to get to their destination productively. To forward packet within a road section, distributed V2V Q-learning (Q-learning occurs between vehicles) combined with QGGF (Q-greedy geographical forwarding) is used for decreasing the delivery delay and the impact of quick vehicle movements on path sensitivity, whereas distributed R2R Q-learning (Q-learning happens between RSU units) is developed for packet forwarding at every intermediate intersection.

Shah *et al.* (2018) recommended a Multi-metric Power Control (MPC) technique, which considers the application needs and channel states to decide a transmit power for safety messages. The MPC provides a best-effort scheme to meet the coverage range demands of a message as the application requires. Also, the concept differentiates among message types to distinguish between coverage. Authors revealed that the best-effort scheme of rendering coverage for various messages can help in congestion control and consequently increase the consciousness by reducing beacon collisions.

Rewadkar & Doye (2018) presented a traffic-aware routing protocol in VANET by the introduction of multi-objective auto-regressive whale optimisation (ARWO) algorithm. ARWO algorithm selects the best path from the multiple paths by considering the multiple objectives, such as end-to-end delay (EED), link life time, packet delay and distance, in the fitness function. Here, the traffic density and the expected average speed of the vehicle are predicted by the exponential weighted moving average approach. The performance of ARWO protocol is compared with four existing techniques, like stable Connected Dominating Set (CDS) based routing protocol, fractional glow worm swarm optimisation, glow worm swarm optimisation, and Whale Optimization Algorithm (WOA), using the metrics, EED, distance, traffic density, and throughput.

Qureshi *et al.* (2020) introduced a distance and signal quality aware routing (DSQR) protocol to manage vehicular networks. The discussed protocol initializes its forwarding decision on the basis of Mid-Area node selection by assessing the direction and distance of neighbour nodes and also considering link quality and chooses the best next forwarder node towards the destination node. The DSQR performance is assessed using vehicle speed and traffic density in practical environment. A Performance comparisons analysis showed the superior performance of discussed protocol in comparison with available protocols and it helps decrease packet drop and link breakage problems.

Bagherlou & Ghaffari (2018) demonstrated a clustering-based reliable routing algorithm for VANETs with robust applications. Here, simulated annealing was utilized for suitable clustering of nodes and the parameters of node degree, coverage and ability were taken into consideration in the proposed technique. To choose cluster head, radial basis function neural network was utilized and an appropriate fitness function with velocity and free buffer size parameters was utilized. Every cluster includes two gateway nodes that are utilized in the form of the communication interface for sending data from one cluster to the other. In Table 2.4 comparison study of coverage aware routing protocols is shown.

Table 2.4 Comparison analysis of coverage aware routing protocols

S.No	Author	Method	Merits	Demerits
1	Darwish *et al.* (2018)	Reliable traffic aware routing protocol	Better received signal strength	Higher mobility leads to more interference rate
2	Bhandari *et al.* (2018)	congestion-aware routing protocol (CoAR)	Better congestion handling More packet delivery ratio	Fuel consumption is not focused

Cont…

S.No	Author	Method	Merits	Demerits
3	Kalogeiton *et al.* (2019)	Geographical aware routing protocol	Increased packet delivery ratio More routing overhead	Higher energy consumption
4	Oubbati *et al.* (2017)	UAV-Assisted VANETs routing protocol	Increased packet delivery ratio Lesser delay	More routing overhead
5	Rashid *et al.* (2020)	Analysed routing based on link stability	Lesser routing overhead Lesser energy consumption	More processing overhead
6	Wu *et al.* (2020)	Q-learning-based Traffic-Aware Routing (QTAR)	Higher average packet delivery ratio Increased throughput	More fuel consumption
7	Shah *et al.* (2018)	Multi-metric Power Control (MPC) approach	Lower transmit power Avoided congestion	More routing overhead
8	Rewadkar & Doye (2018)	traffic-aware routing protocol	More throughput Lesser end to end delay	Decreased network performance with more traffic rate
9	Qureshi *et al.* (2020)	distance and signal quality aware routing (DSQR) protocol	Reduced packet dropping rate Lesser link failure rate	More fuel consumption
10	Bagherlou & Ghaffari	clustering-based reliable routing	More packet delivery ratio	More routing overhead

S.No	Author	Method	Merits	Demerits
	(2018)	algorithm		

2.5 INFERENCE FROM THE EXISTING WORK

The rising progress in this rapid paced society has made vehicles to be the foremost requirement instead of a luxury item. An increase in traffic jams has also been witnessed from then. This rise in traffic jams has been in direct proportion to fuel usage resulting in displeasure and irritation to drivers. VANET (Vehicular Ad Hoc Network) renders efficient and both safer, comfy and robust alternates to the present transportation systems. The important challenges faced in the fuel consumption aware routing in VANET are given as follows:

- Data communication is not focused in the available works which is necessary for rapid decision making with respect to vehicle control, therefore the fuel consumption can be controlled.
- Communication between various SDN agent RSUs existing in multiple layers are hard to be computed owing to coverage problems.
- Successful and robust data transmission is not focused in this technical work that is necessary for efficient decision making due to which routing mechanism is required.

2.6 SUMMARY

In this research work, various technical works has been explained in detail along with its functional procedure and mechanism. This chapter also studies the comparison analysis of the various research approaches in terms of their advantages and drawbacks. This chapter explains the overview of the various research approaches in terms of setbacks and it is concluded from the analysis with the results obtained.

CHAPTER 3

RG TECHNIQUE TO REDUCE THE FUEL CONSUMPTION AND CO_2 EMISSION

3.1 INTRODUCTION

Recently, the problem energy conservation is garnering huge attention in ITS. The current rises in fuel prices also hugely affect the global economy. The drivers are concerned about the fuel consumption not exceeding their monthly budget. Excess usage of petroleum not just makes the budget to increase but also discharge more among pollutants. The Texas A & M Transportation Institute has observed that owing to congestion, urban Americans must travel 5.5 billion hours more and they need to buy an addition 2.9 billion gallons of fuel for a congestion cost of $121 billion whereas 56 billion pounds of additional Carbon Monoxide (CO) and greenhouse gas was emitted into the atmosphere during urban congested conditions just in 2011. The world now is extremely affected by environmental pollution. Therefore, the decrease in fuel consumption can reduce the emission of pollutants and keep the environment clean and green. Even though considerable research has been performed by several researchers in the domain of fuel and energy for alternate fuels, the vehicle industry also has done few efforts to enhance the vehicle modernization for fuel efficiency and economically feasible environment friendly technology.

ITS can be categorized as wire and wireless communications depending on information and electronics technologies combined with transportation system and vehicles. It is a recent approach for the green technology, which not just changes a single vehicle green but also changes the entire group of vehicles green. ITS has already made ripples in the domain of transportation systems. ITS includes a vast array of methods and technologies such in the form of real-time traffic information systems (TIS), electronic toll collection system (ETCS), and automated traffic light control system (ATLCS). It can possibly to develop as the primary tool to resolve surface transportation problems in the next many decades, since an infrastructure is constructed besides physical transportation infrastructure. This system installs communications, control, electronics, and computer technologies for boosting the performance of road transportation systems. ITS technologies are not expectative or futuristic; they are original, is already available in various nations recently, and are present in all countries, which are focused towards their development and deployment.

ITS is a potential technology, which can be utilized for decreasing the fuel consumption and exhaust pollutants that conserves the environment. The technologies mitigate the congestion, render progressed safety, and improve productivity. ITS application is utilized to reduce average distance, travel time, and traffic density estimation. It can be helpful for green purposes by letting the driver know about the best path, which can decrease a considerable amount of fuel since the vehicle's preference is the less congested route.

Vehicles can transmit and receive message with significant data and search for best path as per their location, speed, and direction. A smart vehicle aggregates data utilizing few specific sensors. Once this data is processed, it propagates the information to other vehicles. A major number of vehicles recently run on fossil fuels. Therefore, ITS has to be improved considerably to limit the fuel consumption and also the pollutants which also avoids the global warming and greenhouse gas. The ITS technologies encourage the decrease of fuel consumption with two factors, which is, first to decrease the congestion, helping to maintain optimal speeds in each vehicle and secondly to recommend a green fuel efficient path to the driver.

The vehicular adhoc was established from mobile adhoc network (Rana *et al.* 2020). The VANET utilizes different kinds of communication, which include vehicle to vehicle, vehicle to road side unit and Vehicle to infra structure. These communications require different kinds of sensor and technology (Tiennoy & Saivichit 2018). The VANET utilizes wireless networking technology, which include Wireless Local Area Network (WLAN), WiFi, Zib Bee, LTE (or) Cellular technology, the recent one being Visible Light Communication (VLC) (Mercola 2020). The VANET is devised from Mobile Ad hoc Network (MANET). The Intelligent Vehicle and ADHoc Network was a network in which the storing and monitoring of vehicle data was done(Singh & Kim 2017). It was an ADHoc network, and no specialised communications are required. It utilizes more number of sensors for monitoring the movement of vehicle. Different simulation software exist in the industry, the open source simulation (SUMO) is merged with a network simulator such as Net Sim (or) Network Simulator 2 (NS2) to analyze the VANET performance(Sommer *et al.* 2019).

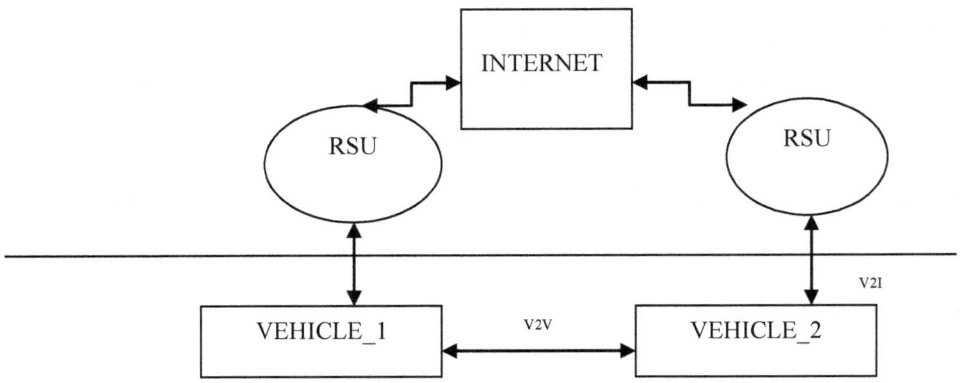

Figure 3.1 Vehicular Adhoc Network Working Model

VANET working is shown in above Figure 3.1. The sample VANET consist only two vehicles that communicating between each other Vehicle to Vehicle (V2V) (Gupta *et al.* 2017). The Vehicles to Infrastructure (V2I) will exchange data from vehicle to infrastructure. The Road Side Unit (RSU) is used to gather the information from vehicles. The RSU used the internet to transmit information from one RSU another (Gao *et al.* 2020). It was developed to reduce the traffic congestion, driver safety, to detect accident etc. The speed governor was used to control the speed of the vehicle near speed breaker, accident zone and used where there is pit in road. This helps to reduce the maintenance of the vehicle.

The vehicles communication takes place between V-V, V-RSU, V-I through Dedicated Short Range Communication (DSRC) (Liu *et al.* 2018). It works in 5.9 MHz bandwidth of 75 MHz and approximate range of 300m. It is developed from Intelligent Transport System (ITS). The VANET uses two different types of models for effective communication. The first one is infrastructure environment, that is permanent connect. The second is Ad Hoc environment, which is a movable environment. Based on these two models, only one VANET is developed (Soleymani *et al.* 2017). The VANET consist of various characteristics, the most promising characteristics are high mobility, rapid changing network topology, predictable mobility, power criteria, time management. The VANET consist of various challenges yet to be solved. They are frequent location changes, congestion control and collision control, frequent signal changes, security.

Finite automata are a mathematical model which accepts the regular language (L). The proposed language L_v (L language, V vehicle). The language L_v consists of set of stings w_1, w_2,....w_n.. The designed finite automata will check whether string is going to accept or not. $L_v=\{v^+\}$ $L_v=\{v,vv,vvv,......\}$. The language L_v is developed for the VANET. It assists in developing FA model and calculations are carried out for traffic reduction, fuel consumption and CO_2 emission.

In this work, ReGrouping (RG) technique is proposed which will condense the fuel utilization of assorted vehicles in VANET. The CO_2 emission and traffic level in the scrupulous direction are reduced. VANET representation is urbanized using Finite Automata (FA). From the FA model the VANET constructed.

3.2 FUEL CONSUMPTION IN VANET

In this work, ReGrouping (RG) technique is proposed which will condense the fuel utilization of assorted vehicles in VANET. The CO_2 emission and traffic level in the scrupulous direction are reduced. VANET representation was urbanized using Finite Automata (FA). From the FA model, the VANET is constructed based on traffic information. Traffic information system is very important for ITS application. The information about the number of vehicles in the road is very important to eliminate the traffic congestion. The traffic information system gathers the traffic data and transmits this data to the driver in the roads. In VANET, every vehicle periodically exchanges information every 300 ms. The traffic density is the most influential factor that affects the average speed of the vehicle. ITS application performance depends on how accurately it can measure the traffic flow rate, traffic density, and mean speed of the vehicle. VANET is a high mobility network.

3.3 VEHICULAR NETWORK MODEL

A VANET generally includes vehicles, RSUs, and TA, as illustrated in Figure 3.2.

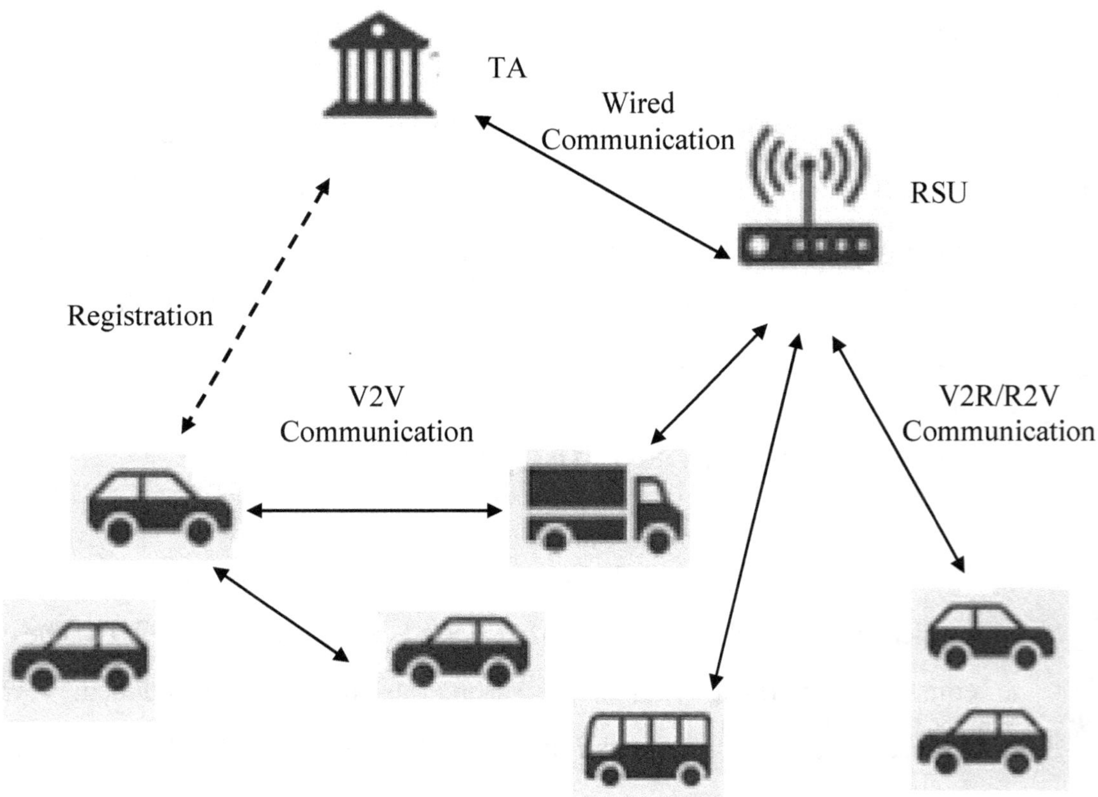

Figure 3.2 The Network Architecture of VANET

Trusted Authority acts as an administrator in VANET and is involved with the authentication management of network nodes, which include vehicles and RSUs. To get attached to the VANET, each of the nodes should undergo registration by themselves at TA in prior. Owing to the movement of vehicles, an often changing set of vehicles, which needs TA to yield real-time registration service through secure network architecture is considered. On the contrary, the locations and the overall number of RSUs generally remain unmodified for a considerably longer duration. The registration of RSUs can be completed during initialization stage. In addition, TA has a list of registered vehicles and is responsible for disclosing the actual identities of malicious vehicles and cancelling the licenses of these vehicles in time. RSUs in the form of roadside infrastructure are distributed all around the area of TA. Communication between RSU and TA depends on wired channel whereas RSU communicates with vehicles through wireless channel with the help of DSRC protocol. RSUs relay messages not just between TA and vehicles but also between vehicles. A RSU and set of vehicles registered under RSU will form a subgroup of VANET. Vehicles, which enter new into the transmission range of RSU must get authenticated by RSU. Each vehicle is fitted with OBU to have communication with other entities in VANET and use DSRC protocol. Realistic TPD is also included in vehicle. It can temporarily store the confidential information and associated computation service, which is more practical compared to ideal TPD, which never reveals any secrets. Hence, the secrets saved in TPD must be updated periodically with the help of TA.

3.4 FINITE AUTOMATA

The FA concept results in making the VANET for intelligent routing. The FA doesn't permit any other string, which does not exist in the language and will move into the accepting state. The VANET will operate in the same way. The merits of Finite automata are listed below:

- Finite state machines are flexible.
- Easy to move from a significant abstract to a code execution.

- Low processor overhead.
- Easy determination of reachability of a state.

Regrouping technique introduced in this work can perform better VANET routing with reduced fuel consumption by adapting the finite automate procedure for route path construction.

3.4.1 Finite Automata

Finite Automata (FA) is the easiest machine for pattern identification. The finite automata or finite state machine is an abstract machine that includes five elements or tuple. It consists of a set of states and rules for changing from one state to the other but it relies on the input symbol used. Fundamentally, it is an abstract framework of digital computer. The figure below illustrates few important features of a common automation.

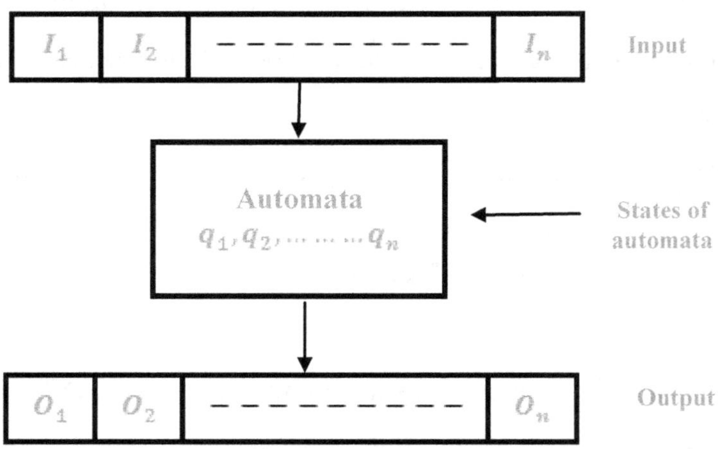

Figure 3.3 Features of Finite automata

The above Figure 3.3 shows following features of automata:

1. Input
2. Output

3. States of automata
4. State relation
5. Output relation

A Finite Automata consists of the following :

Q : Finite set of states.

Σ : set of Input Symbols.

q : Initial state.

F : set of Final States.

δ : Transition Function.

In this work, deterministic finite automata is used for graph construction. DFA consists of 5 tuples {Q, Σ, q, F, δ}.

Q : set of all states.

Σ : set of input symbols. (Symbols which machine takes as input)

q : Initial state. (Starting state of a machine)

F : set of final state.

δ : Transition Function, defined as δ : Q X Σ --> Q.

In a DFA, for a particular input character, the machine goes to one state only per single transition. A transition function is defined on every state for every input symbol. Also in DFA null (or ε) move is not allowed, i.e., DFA cannot change state without any input character. For example, Figure 3.4 shown below has Σ = {0, 1} which accepts all strings ending with 0.

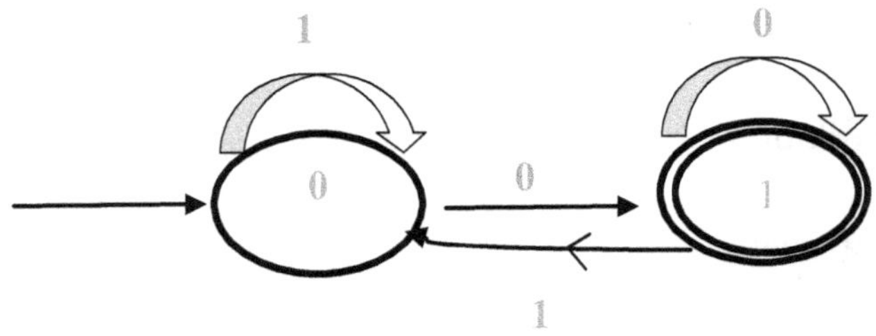

Figure 3.4 DFA with $\Sigma = \{0, 1\}$

One important thing to note is, there can be many possible DFAs for a pattern. A DFA with minimum number of states is generally preferred.

3.4.2 Finite Automate Construction for Registered Vehicles

The vehicle that is not registered in our network, will not use our network. The vehicle, which is registered in our VANET, is allowed to reach the destination and utilize the benefits. As a result, security of the VANET network is improved. FA model is designed and it is given below.

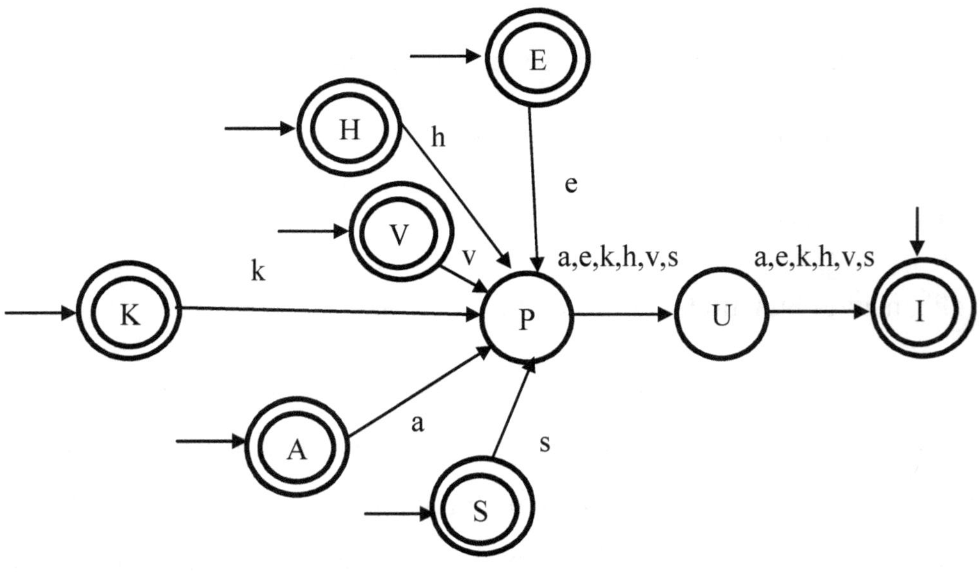

Figure 3.5 Finite Automata Model without Regrouping (RG) Technique

To create the VANET, the locations were identified and shown in the Figure 3.5. The states were named as K,H,S,A,V,E,P,U,I that was specified as set of states in FA($Q,\sum,q,q_{f},\delta$) in which nodes (K,H,S,A,V,E,K,I) can function as starting node and also accepting node. This VANET was especially developed for Educational Institutions (EI). Every EI includes several vehicles in which each one will consider several students for different position. The students those who were travelling in similar lane were selected. Hence, vehicles moving in same path (K to I) were chosen for developing the VANET. The vehicles must enrol in the network so that the advantages can be reaped. Every Educational Institutions Vehicle (EIV) begins at different places, were dropping the students in different places. In the network at convinced end, number of students will be condensed by 50% and only some were reaching the destination node from each EIV. In the network, it was observed that all the vehicles in a scrupulous lane were getting to the same node in the VANET. A new idea Regrouping (RG) approach is proposed. Regrouping is a means of moving the students from one bus to the other. With the help of RG, students of different EIV were moved from one EIV to another so that the number of EIV can be reduced. The persons moving towards same location was found in the VANET and it was also observed that the overall strength is decreased by 50% in every EVI at ReGrouping Point (RGP). RGP in the VANET is node P.

Table 3.1 Transition Table

States/Input	a	e	k	h	v	s
A⟶	P	-	-	-	-	-
E	-	P	-	-	-	-
K	-	-	P	-	-	-
H	-	-	-	P	-	-
V	-	-	-	-	P	-
S	-	-	-	-	-	S
P	U	U	U	U	U	U
U	I	I	I	I	I	I
*I	-	-	-	-	-	-

The above transition Table 3.1 was derived for the corresponding Figure 3.5. The transition table contains the various states in which the finite automata were going to travel. The inputs given to the finite automata model were the various EIV. The input to the model starts from node K, V, A, S, H, and E reaches the node P. The node P is a common point in the network for all the EIV. From node P, the inputs will travel through the node U and it will reach the destination node I.

In the transition Table 3.1, it is found that the functions had been executed at every node. The input provided to every node and the corresponding operations are given in the table. The different transition functions from every starting to destination node are obtained.

The transition function for different states (nodes in VANET) is provided as follows

$\delta(A,a)=P$, $\delta(A,e)=\phi$, $\delta(A,k)= \phi$, $\delta(A,h)= \phi$, $\delta(A,v)= \phi$, $\delta(A,s)= \phi$

Create the node A, the starting point is A and every input is verified sequentially. For A,a, it moves to the node P. Later, the rest of the input stays in the same state, hence it is labelled as ϕ.

$\delta(E,a)=\phi$, $\delta(E,e)=P$, $\delta(E,k)=\phi$, $\delta(E,h)=\phi$, $\delta(E,v)=\phi$, $\delta(E,s)=\phi$

Create the node E, the starting point is E and every input is verified sequentially. For E,e it moves to the node P. Later, the rest of the input stays in the same state, hence it is labelled as ϕ.

$\delta(K,a)=\phi$, $\delta(K,e)=\phi$, $\delta(K,k)=P$, $\delta(K,h)=\phi$, $\delta(K,v)=\phi$, $\delta(K,s)=\phi$

Create the node K, the starting point is K and every input is verified sequentially. For K,k it moves to the node P. Later, the rest of the input stays in the same state, hence it is labelled as ϕ.

$\delta(H,a)=\phi$, $\delta(H,e)=\phi$, $\delta(H,k)=\phi$, $\delta(H,h)=P$, $\delta(H,v)=\phi$, $\delta(H,s)=\phi$

Create the node H, the starting point is H and every input is verified sequentially. For H,h it moves to the node P. Later, the rest of the input stays in the same state, hence it is labelled as ϕ.

$\delta(V,a)=\phi$, $\delta(V,e)=\phi$, $\delta(V,k)=\phi$, $\delta(V,h)=\phi$, $\delta(V,v)=P$, $\delta(V,s)=\phi$

Create the node V, the starting point is V and every input is verified sequentially. For V,v it moves to the node P. Later, the rest of the input stays in the same state, hence it is labelled as ϕ.

$\delta(S,a)=\phi$, $\delta(S,e)=\phi$, $\delta(S,k)=\phi$, $\delta(S,h)=\phi$, $\delta(S,v)=\phi$, $\delta(S,s)=P$

From the node V, the starting point is V and each input is checked one by one. For S,s it moves to the node P. Then the rest of the input remained in the same state therefore, it is marked as ϕ.

$\delta(P,a)= U$, $\delta(P,e)=U$, $\delta(P,k)= U$, $\delta(P,h)= U$, $\delta(P,v)= U$, $\delta(P,s)= U$

From the node P, each input is checked one by one. For P,a,e,s,k,h,v it moves to the node U.

$\delta(U,a)= I$, $\delta(U,e)=I$, $\delta(U,k)= I$, $\delta(U,h)= I$, $\delta(U,v)= I$, $\delta(U,s)= I$

From the node U, each input is checked one by one. For P,a,e,s,k,h,v it moves to the node I.

$\delta(I,a)= \phi$, $\delta(I,e)=\phi$, $\delta(I,k)= \phi$, $\delta(I,h)= \phi$, $\delta(I,v)= \phi$, $\delta(I,s)= \phi$

The node I is the destination node, therefore there is no more transitions. From the above transition function, it can able to drive a common transition function.

$$\delta(\text{states,input})= P \textbf{ Union } \delta(\text{states,input})= U \textbf{ Union } \delta(\text{states,input})= I$$

$$\delta(X,w)= P \quad \delta(X,w)= U \; \mathbf{U} \; \delta(X,w)= I$$

$$\sum \delta(X,w)= P \; \mathbf{U} \; \delta(X,w)=I \qquad (3.1)$$

where w={a,e,k,h,v,s}

Table 3.2 Using Equation the Formulas Derived

S.NO	Terms	Description	Formula
1	D	**D_EIV**	∑ D i=1 to n
2	C	**CO_2_EIV**	∑ C i=1 to n
3	M	**C_EIV**	∑ M i=1 to n
4	F	**F_EIV**	∑ F i=1 to n

- **D_EIV**→Distance travelled by Educational Institution Vehicle
- **CO_2_EIV** → **CO_2**(2640 grams per/liter) emitted by Educational Institution Vehicle
- **C_EIV** →Cost spend on fuel by Educational Institution Vehicle
- **F_EIV** →Fuel used by Educational Institution Vehicle

The designed VANET consist of various EIV. In the proposed model, all the EIV are made to start at various node and travel towards the same destination. In the Table 3.2, various EIV travel distance from their starting node to destination node are calculated. The Table 3.3 shows the fuel consumed, distance travelled by each EIV and CO_2 emitted by each EIV.

Table 3.3 VANET without RG Technique (per day)

NODE	EIV_K	EIV_H	EIV_S	EIV_V	EIV_A	EIV_E	Total
D_EIV	95	94	90	86.3	88	83	536.3
F_EIV	15.8	15.6	15	14.3	14.6	13.8	89.1
CO_2_EIV	41712	41184	39600	37752	38544	36432	235224
C_EIV	1106	1092	1050	1001	1022	966	6237

The below Table 3.4 shows the fuel consumed, distance travelled, CO_2 emitted by each EIV for one-week travel while considering 5 days as working days.

Table 3.4 VANET without RG Technique (per week)

NODE	EIV_K	EIV_H	EIV_S	EIV_V	EIV_A	EIV_E	Total
D_EIV	950	940	900	863	880	830	3563
F_EIV	158	156	150	143	146	138	591
CO_2_EIV	417120	411840	396000	377520	385440	364320	1560240
C_EIV	11060	10920	10500	10010	10220	9660	41370

3.5 REGROUPING TECHNIQUE

Regrouping approach was useful to decrease the fuel consumption, distance travelled by every EIV, CO_2 discharged from every EIV. The finite automata after the implementation of RG approach have been developed and it is illustrated in below Figure 3.6.

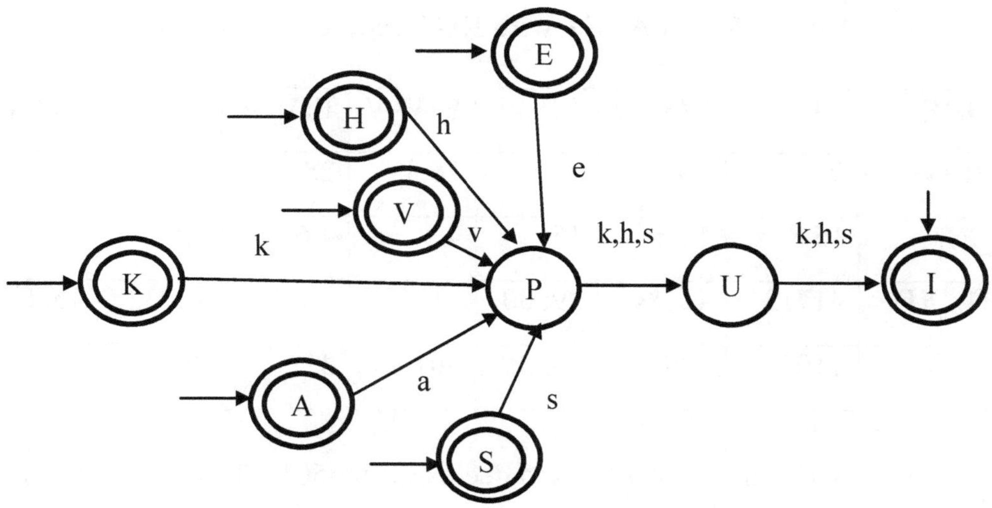

Figure 3.6 Finite Automata Model with RG Technique

The above Figure 3.6 is designed with RG technique. The core concept in the VANET was to limit the number of EIV employing regrouping approach at node RGP (P). In the FA model given above, the EIV travelling from RGP (P) to the destination was decreased by 50%. Consequently, the number of EIV was decreased by half. It was shown up in the fuel consumption, CO_2 emission and maintenance. From RGP (P), it has been reduced to 3 EIV. The distance for every EIV, CO_2, fuel consumption is computed for single way travel. The result was illustrated in Table 3.5.

$$\sum \delta(X,w1) = P \cup \delta(X,w2) = I \tag{3.2}$$

where w1={a,e,k,h,v,s}, w2={k,h,s}

S=Total no of students in each EIV

N=S/2

$$\mathbf{RG_v = \sum N} \tag{3.3}$$

where i=1 to n

Table 3.5 VANET with RG Technique (per day)

NODE	EIV_K	EIV_H	EIV_S	EIV_V	EIV_A	EIV_E	Total
D_EIV	95	94	90	26.3	28	23	356.3
F_EIV	15.8	15.6	15	4.3	4.6	3.8	59.1
CO_2_EIV	41712	41184	39600	11352	12144	10032	156024
C_EIV	1106	1092	1050	301	322	266	4137

The number of EIV was decreased by 50%. Table 3.6 illustrates the Km travelled, fuel consumed, CO_2 discharged by every EIV for one-week trip with 5 days taken as working day. Owing to the decrease in EIV traffic from RGP to destination, some amount of traffic has been reduced during busy hours.

Table 3.6 VANET with RG Technique (per week)

NODE	EIV_K	EIV_H	EIV_S	EIV_V	EIV_A	EIV_E	Total
D_EIV	950	940	900	263	280	230	5363
F_EIV	158	156	150	43	46	38	891
CO_2_EIV	417120	411840	396000	113520	121440	100320	2352240
C_EIV	11060	10920	10500	3010	3220	2660	62370

3.6 RESULTS AND DISCUSSION

Experimentation is done using 64 -bit Ubuntu 12.04 operating system having Intel Core i7-2670QM processor @ 2.20 GHz and RAM of 8 GB. The network simulator tool used is NS2.34. The Table 3.7 shows the comparison of Km travelled, fuel consumed, cost for fuel, CO_2 emitted before and after RG techniques for one week (5 working days). The comparative graph was shown in Figure 3.7.

Table 3.7 Overall Comparison Per Week

OVERALL COMPARISON PER WEEK			
NODE	**Without RG Technique**	**With RG Technique**	**Difference**
D_EIV	5363	3563	1800
F_EIV	891	591	300
CO_2_EIV	2352240	1560240	792000
C_EIV	62370	41370	21000

Complete analyzes about distance comparison of each node before and after RG technique was shown in Table 3.8. It was clear from the results that D_EIV total after RG is 3563 and before RG is 5363. Figure 3.7 confirms that distance covered after RG is very low than distance covered before RG. It confirms that with the usage of ReGrouping technique, there is no requirement for unnecessary distance travel, thereby reducing the fuel consumption, CO_2 emission and cost.

Table 3.8 Distance Comparison

DISTANCE COMPARISON							
NODE	**EIV_K**	**EIV_H**	**EIV_S**	**EIV_V**	**EIV_A**	**EIV_E**	**Total**
D_EIV After RG Technique	950	940	900	263	280	230	3563
D_EIV Before RG Technique	950	940	900	863	880	830	5363

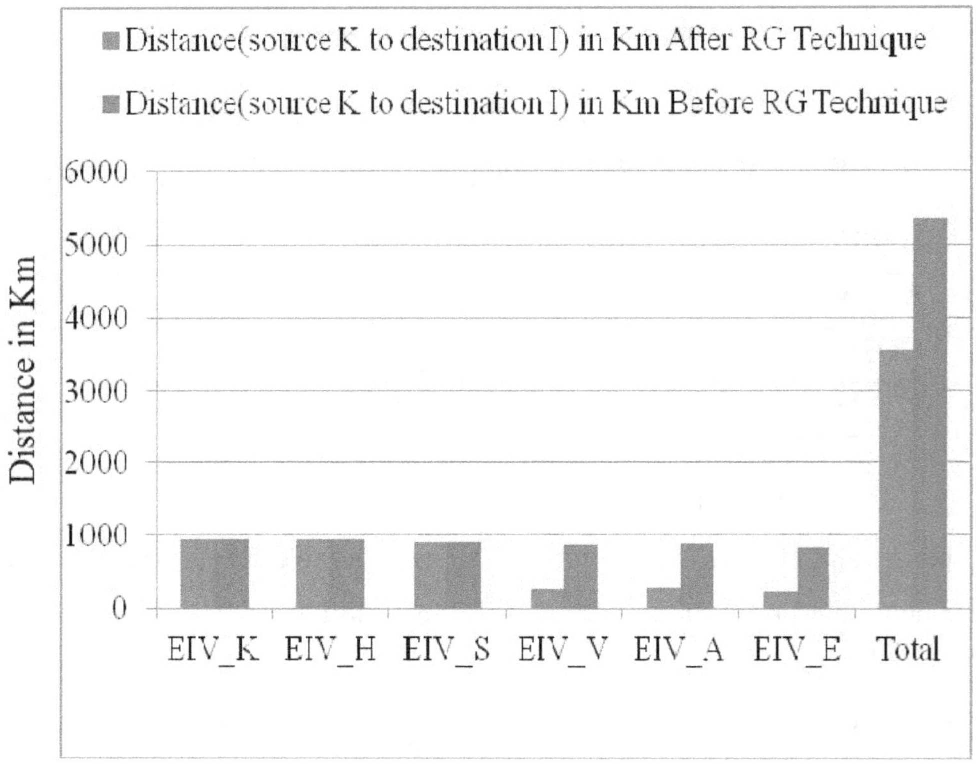

Figure 3.7 Distance Comparison

The comparison of fuel consumption of each node before and after RG technique was shown in Table 3.9. It was understandable from the results that F_EIV total after RG was 591 and before RG is 891. Figure 3.8 further points out that the fuel consumption before RG is extremely high than fuel consumption after RG. It reassures that with the assistance of ReGrouping technique, there is no necessity for needless fuel consumption, thereby reducing the CO_2 emission, distance travel and cost too.

Table 3.9 Fuel Consumption Comparison

FUEL CONSUMPTION COMPARISON							
NODE	**EIV_K**	**EIV_H**	**EIV_S**	**EIV_V**	**EIV_A**	**EIV_E**	**Total**
F_EIV After RG Technique	158	156	150	43	46	38	591
F_EIV Before RG Technique	158	156	150	143	146	138	891

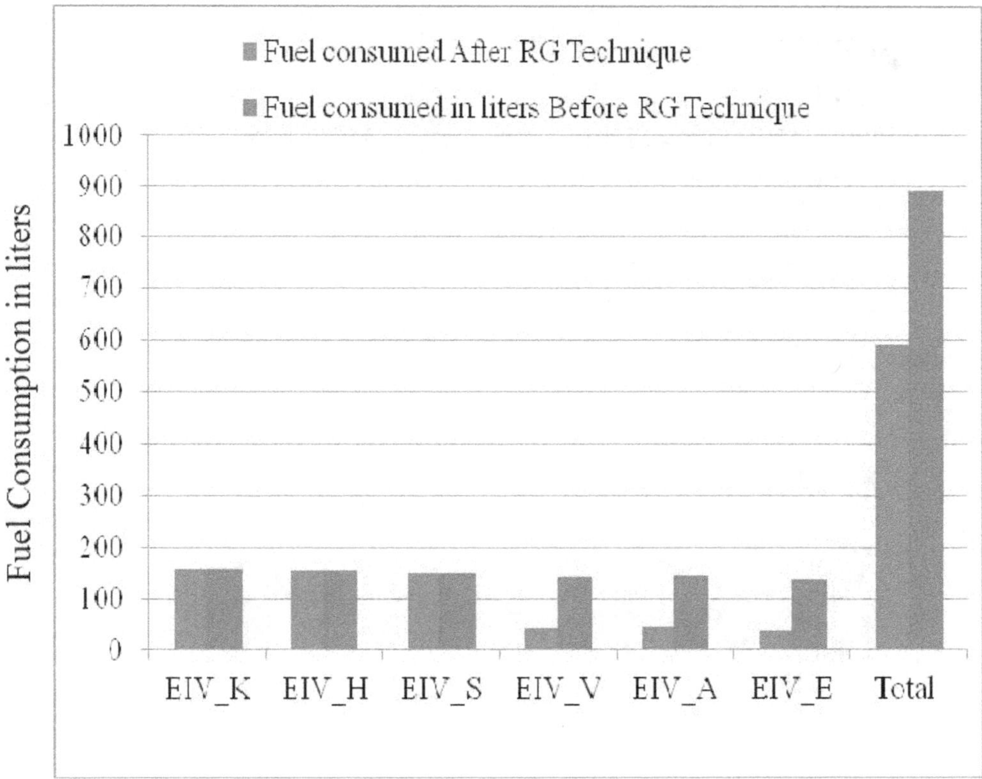

Figure 3.8 Fuel Consumption Comparison

Table 3.10 provides the comparison of CO_2 of each node before and after RG technique. It is obvious from the results that CO_2_EIV total after RG is 1560240 and before RG is 2352240. Figure 3.9 further assures that the CO_2 emission before RG is very lesser when comparing against the CO_2 emission after RG. It declares that with the practice of ReGrouping technique, the CO_2 emission is considerably reduced.

Table 3.10 CO_2 (2640 grams per/liter) Comparison

CO_2(2640 grams per/liter) COMPARISON							
NODE	**EIV_K**	**EIV_H**	**EIV_S**	**EIV_V**	**EIV_A**	**EIV_E**	**Total**
CO_2_EIV After RG Technique	417120	411840	396000	113520	121440	100320	1560240
CO_2_EIV Before RG Technique	417120	411840	396000	377520	385440	364320	2352240

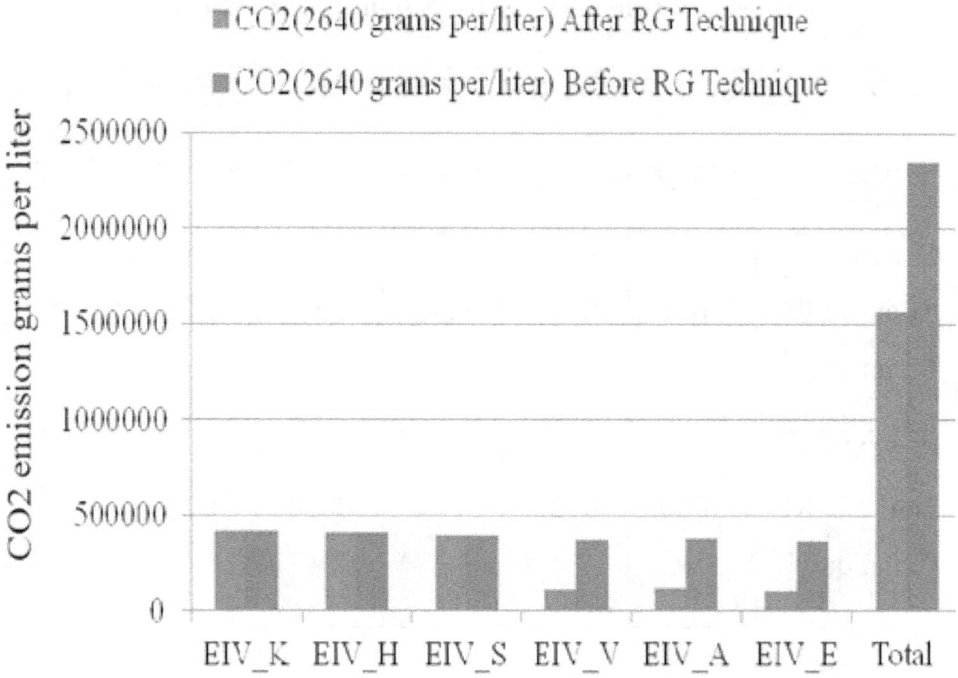

Figure 3.9 CO_2 (2640 grams per/liter) Comparison

The cost saving comparison of each node before and after RG technique was shown in Table 3.11. It is clear from the results that C_EIV total after RG is 41370 and before RG are 62370. Figure 3.10 confirms that the cost before RG is extremely high than cost after RG. It reassures that with the assistance of ReGrouping technique, there is no necessity for additional cost.

Table 3.11 Cost Saving Comparison

COST SAVING COMPARISON USING RG TECHNIQUE(in rupees)							
NODE	**EIV_K**	**EIV_H**	**EIV_S**	**EIV_V**	**EIV_A**	**EIV_E**	**Total**
C_EIV After RG Technique	11060	10920	10500	3010	3220	2660	41370
C_EIV Before RG Technique	11060	10920	10500	10010	10220	9660	62370

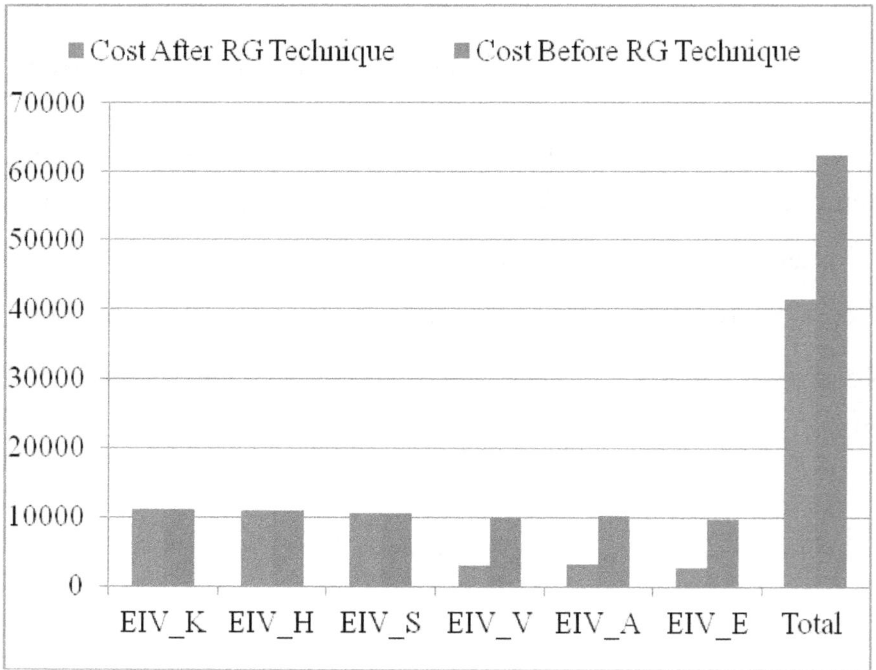

Figure 3.10 Cost Saving Comparison using RG Technique

3.7 SUMMARY

In this technical work, different works have been surveyed to learn the functioning of VANET. In this, a Finite automata framework is proposed for developing the VANET. With this model, several formulas has been derived for computing the fuel consumed by different vehicles, CO_2 emission from several vehicles, and the traffic decrease during peak hour. In addition, the fuel, CO_2 and traffic level is calculated per week.

CHAPTER 4

FUEL CONSUMPTION AND DELAY AWARE TRAFFIC SCHEDULING IN VANET

4.1 INTRODUCTION

In wireless and vehicular technology, vehicular ad hoc networks (VANETs) was a predominant research subject owing to no-infrastructure communication technology required in Intelligent Transportation Systems (ITS), increase in the number of vehicles on road and regular movement of humans (Akabane *et al.* 2017). Ameliorating the traffic congestion was highlighted in improving ITS for decreasing the fuel usage and pollutant discharge, traffic safety improvement and rendering mobile infotainment to passengers. This is performed by make the vehicles know about its environment and improving on-road communication (Condurat *et al.* 2017).

Intelligent and vehicular communication must be improved for rendering significant safety and non-safety demands of communication in VANET scenarios(Omar *et al.* 2016). Communication between vehicles and the neighboring roadside equipment that were installed was facilitated in mobile ad hoc network (MANET), which is a subcategory of VANET. Different models including vehicle-to-infrastructure (V2I) and vehicle-to-vehicle (V2V) exist in VANET communications (Dey *et al.* 2016). Due to the fast paced growth of vehicular communications, different studies are put forward which include routing protocols offering improved performance and also suitability to changes in network topology, VANET-LTE integration, improvement of latency and robustness, constraints of privacy and security, design of medium-access-layer (MAC) procedures that is flexible and modelling of channel (Mourad *et al.* 2017). In the case of ad hoc networks, it was vital to include routing protocols. Initialization and maintenance of routes were carried out with the help of those routing protocols for enabling multi-hop communication and also extending the network's service field(Jiang & Han 2018).

In VANET, messages generated from vehicles were adhoc and intermittent in nature. To permit the vehicles to be connected to the out-of-transmission range road-side unit (RSU), Vehicle-to-vehicle (V2V) communication of multi-hop fashion is usually considered (Taleb 2018). In order to assist a type of applications such as, e.g., car accident alert, road condition warning, video streaming, web browsing, and file sharing, V2V through multi-hop transmission provides bursty data flows to a vehicle at a distance(Dighriri *et al.* 2018). Eventhough multi-hop V2V mode can considerably increase the connectivity probability, end-to-end delay and single hop delay affect the quality of service (QoS) of the vehicular communication and may result in reduced network throughput. According to the users' view, end-to-end delay and single hop delay were the most crucial factors and were commonly the most essential service demands since they directly depict their experiences and degree of satisfaction. Therefore, a thorough knowledge of the single hop queuing performance of various kinds of data is necessary. But, the way to evaluate the multi-hop end-to-end delay and single hop delay under queuing bound condition is still a huge challeng due to the burst data traffic features and extremely dynamic channel environments.

In vehicular network, important limitations and features such as low bandwidth, interference and nodes mobility are taken into consideration for the design of routing protocols of VANET (Wahid *et al.* 2018). Dynamic topology exists in VANET, which provide support to any kind of application during run time (Khaliq *et al.* 2017). Constant research has been carried out for improving routing decisions by taking the VANETs challenges and drawbacks.

The routing protocols of VANET (Taleb 2018) are classified based on predictive mobility and power-sensitive abilities. This categorizes the protocols in accordance with the improvement of quality-of-service (QoS) and efficient usage of resources (Dighriri *et al.* 2018). Centralized control is rendered with the help of cluster-based routing protocols in this regard and in highly dense networks, saturation is prevented while using those protocols. Position information or topology based low-latency application protocols are also developed (Ahmad & Shcherbakov 2018). To compute optimum protocol from different techniques, parameters such as interference, low collision, security, end-to end delay are utilized, which guarantee robust QoS routing.

The rapid delivery of Traffic information is an important objective of intelligent transport applications. They also permit coordinated processing of vehicles information for improving traffic detection accuracy and effectiveness. They intently monitor the traffic pattern for traffic management and they are again categorized as, "Monitoring of Traffic, Management of Traffic, Platooning, Tracking of Vehicle, Services for Notification". VANET applications associated with the comfort of the passenger who are travelling in vehicle are called as comfort applications. It is again grouped as, "Management of parking place, Distributed games and/or talks, Peer to Peer applications".

The main motivation of the research work is to achieve the delay reduced data communication, thus the decision regarding traffic management can be taken fastly which would lead to greater fuel consumption reduction.

This is done by introducing the Fuel Consumption and Delay aware Traffic Scheduling Method (FCD-TSM) method. In this research work, when vehicle is encountered with another vehicle for the data communication then it will communicate with the road side units and gain information such as vehicles count present in area and coverage region locations. To ensure the successful data transmission in this work coverage aware clustering protocol is introduced which would ensure the successful data transmission. Based on nodes count present within cluster message replication quota is decided which reduce the network load and ensures the successful data transmission.

4.2 INFORMATION GATHERING FROM ROAD SIDE UNITS

Static RSU (Stat-RSU) is deployed as a communication node on sides of road for collecting and processing traffic information, which is termed as Roadside Unit Driven Data Communication Network (RU-DCN). Without connecting to any processing centre or data collection centre, Stat-RSU is working as a static node. Transmission range of Stat-RSU is similar to nodes deployed in vehicle-to vehicle (V2V).

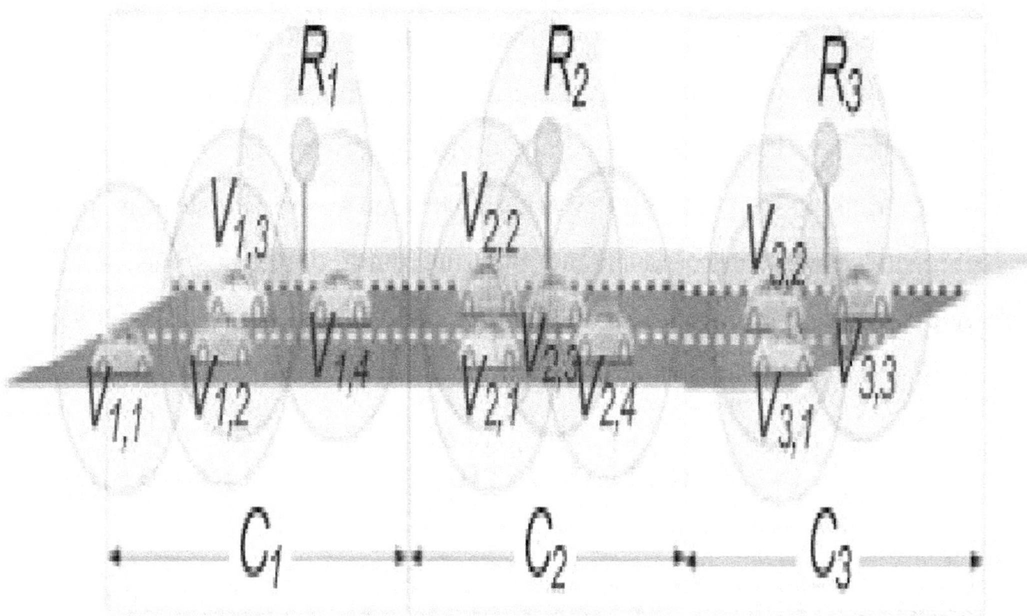

Figure 4.1 RU-DCN Network

N cells are formed by dividing the road as shown in Figure 4.1. Where, n represents cell index and there exist one Stat-RSU in every cell, R_n represents Stat-RSU in cell n, vehicle i in cell n is represented as $V_{n,i}$. GPS is used to obtain the locations of the vehicles. There exist 4 classes of messages in proposed protocol, which are extended from architecture of DCN.

- A polling message: It is broadcasted by Stat-RSU periodically to all vehicles in same cell.
- A data $d_{n,i}$ text it message: It is a message of $V_{n,i}$ in R_n, which is sent to Stat-RSU after the reception of polling message. The data $d_{n,i}$ represents ith vehicles velocity and direction.
- A request info. message: It is a vehicle message sends to Stat-RSU for requesting traffic information of it.

- A reply info. message: It is a Stat-RSU reply message to vehicle, after the reception of request info. Message

The packets add the source's position and roadside segment (RSU ID) to request the ''Interest'' message toward the direction of the desired data. The structure of polling message and request info. message are similar to the ''Interest'' message of the legacy NDN, and the structures of data dn,i message and reply info. message are also similar to the ''Data'' message of the legacy NDN. The structure of packets is provided in Table 4.1.

Table 4.1 Packet Header Structure

Types/Packet	Polling	Data	Request Info	Reply Info
Name selector	Polling Node Selector	Polling RSU ID	Traffic RSU ID	Traffic Node selector
Guilders position	Conditions Position	Conditions Position	Conditions Position	Conditions Position
Time stamp	Time stamp	Time stamp	Time stamp	Time stamp
Signature	NONCE	Signature	NONCE	Signature

Each name prefix exhibits a hierarchical name format, and the ''/'' character indicates a delimiter among various elements. The naming convention for polling message→ ''/polling/node selector/conditions/ position/timestamp/NONCE'' is as below

- ''Polling'' finds an application to create a name for the polling message.
- ''Node selector'' finds a node of resource data when SA-RSU gathers the traffic information in the road section.
- ''Conditions'' helps to identify the details of the incidents including detection, speed, lane and segment.

- ‘‘Position’’ used to identify a position of the content source.
- ‘‘Timestamp’’ helpful to identify the time of occurrence of the event.
- ‘‘NONCE’’ identifies every distinct ‘‘Interest’’ message to avert the loops in the network.

In VANET, modified DCN protocols process is explained with the installation of Stat-RSU and it is called as RU-DCN network. ‘‘Interest’’ message’s prefix is declared by each Stat-RSU for announcing the traffic information. There are two operation modes in proposed data distribution protocol, which are, active and broadcast mode.

4.2.1 BROADCAST MODE

Each Stat-RSU broadcast a periodical polling message for gathering information during the beginning of protocol. Name prefix structure is known through the data collection process, which in turn is a polling prefix. Polling message is transmitted by requester node to vehicles present in their cell. Timer is fixed by each vehicle that gets the polling message in Stat-RSU’s identical transmission range as per the distance between Stat-RSU and polling message is relayed by the vehicle at a distance to Stat-RSU’s next hop.

Take vehicles $V_{1,2}$ and $V_{1,3}$ present in the roadside unit R_1’s transmission range edge. This roadside unit will transmit a polling message to every vehicle within their range of transmission. In the next hop, the received polling message is relayed by forwarder nodes $V_{1,2}$ and $V_{1,3}$ to the remaining vehicles. Later, next forwarder nodes is given by $V_{1,1}$ and $V_{1,4}$. Vehicle $V_{1,2}$is waiting to receive data $d_{1,1}$ from $V_{1,1}$ and Vehicle $V_{1,3}$ is waiting to receive data $d_{1,4}$ from $V_{1,4}$. This will continue until $V_{1,1}$ and $V_{1,4}$ are not capable of forwarding the polling messages to any vehicles. When $V_{1,1}$ and $V_{1,4}$ transmits $d_{1,1}$ and $d_{1,4}$ to $V_{1,2}$ and $V_{1,3}$, $V_{1,2}$ and $V_{1,3}$ will add their data along with the received data as $d_{1,1}$ + $d_{1,2}$ and $d_{1,4}$ + $d_{1,3}$, in a piggy-back pattern before transmitting them back to R_1. The format of data is illustrated in Figure 4.2.

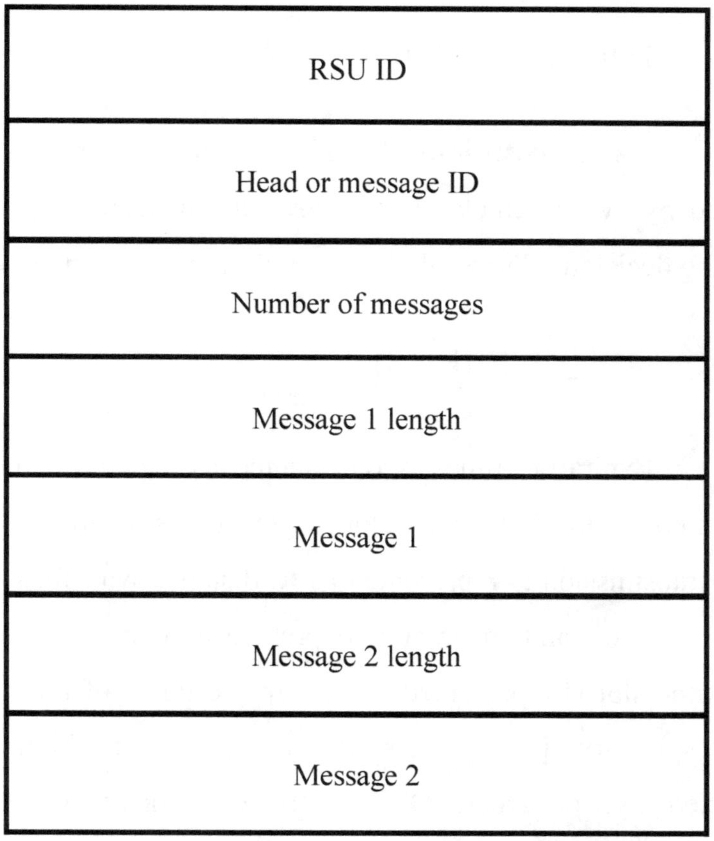

Figure 4.2 Structure of the data $d_{n,i}$ message

4.2.2 ACTIVE MODE

Request info. Message is sent by vehicle, when it requires information from Stat-RSU, identified as a RSU ID/traffic prefix of a Stat-RSU. In case, the vehicle along the path is not saving reply info. Message, requesting vehicle is sent with a reply info. Message by Stat-RSU. In each vehicle, the decision process gets executed. Timer is fixed by a vehicles that gets request info. Message depending on distance between last hop vehicle. Request info. Message gets forwarded by the vehicle at the farthest distance among all the vehicles, until that reply info is maintained. Message's cached copy in any node or Stat-RSU.

4.2.3 FORWARDING DECISION

For request info. Message, distance metrics computation is performed by every vehicle. Timer-based mechanism is applied for making forwarding decisions. Timer of expiration is calculated using Eq 4.1,

$$T_{slot} = \left\lfloor \frac{R - d}{R} \right\rfloor \times (t_{max} - t) + t \tag{4.1}$$

Expiration timer is represented as T_{slots}, which is expressed as time slots count. In MAC layer, slot length time is identical to this. Radius of wireless transmission is represented as R, distance with forwarder position is represented as d, random timer is expressed as t, in MAC layer, maximum waiting time slot is represented as t_{max}. In the range of transmission, request info. Message or polling message along with position information is broadcasted by forwarder. Distance between position of forwarder and receiver is computed by receiver.

Then all vehicle's expiry time is calculated. Expiration timer t in the range $[0, t_d]$, is set by the vehicles moving towards Stat-RSU in a random manner. Expiration timer t is set with a value greater than t_d by remaining vehicles. t_d corresponds to the distance comparison's threshold time between Stat-RSU and vehicle. Therefore, farther vehicle from forwarder needs to wait with a shorter period than a nearby forwarder. It indicates that, T_{slots} is small when R is near to d. Request info. or polling message is rebroadcasted by vehicle, if timer expires. Request info. Or polling message is discarded in other vehicles if they receive same packet and timer is stopped.

4.3 COVERAGE AWARE CLUSTERING PROTOCOL

In a vehicular network having area A, suppose that N nodes were installed in random. The coverage area of single vehicular node was given by a(n). For each vehicle, disk coverage model is used everywhere in this work. At node n , a(n) is disk centred with coverage range radius Rs. N nodes network coverage is denoted as N_n=1 a(n) and network coverage ratio is derived with Eq 4.2,

$$p(N) = \frac{(\cup_{n=1}^{N} a(n)) \cap A}{A} \quad (4.2)$$

Initially, the network is deployed with active and alive nodes and it was presume to have the whole area covered, that is ρ(N)=1. With ρth ≤ 1, relaxed coverage constraint may be derived as at times full coverage was an extremely significant constraint.

4.3.1 Information Update

During the network initialization phase, information was updated the foremost, where each node within 2Rs range will exchange its information on energy and its position with its neighbours. Network localization technique or GPS unit was utilized by every node to be aware of their information on its own position. This was a supposition and it is truly and practically feasible since different algorithms for localization were designed with improved accuracy. There was no surety of whole coverage area, when the information about position of nodes was not accessible. However, by statistical means, it can be ensured. This was because of the fact that, sleep node having no information on the location, will not be capable of guaranteeing the coverage of every points in its coverage region.

4.3.2 Cluster Head Selection

Cluster Head (CH) organizes the inter-/intra-cluster information traffic and packets transmission. Efficient performance of network combined with robustness was ensured by the right cluster election. Depending on velocity or location, CH was selected in a majority of the protocols on cluster routing. It was not optimal to select the CH on the basis of location, since the location of the chosen vehicles may vary based on its relative speed through the network with regard to other vehicles.

It is reported that, vehicle with better location information may be undesirable for rapid selection of CH. In several conditions, velocity based CH selection was also a right preference since the relative motion of vehicle may also quite more. There may be cluster Instability experienced. The speed of vehicles influence the locations of vehicles. To accomplish better reliability of network and stability of cluster, several aspects has to be taken into consideration while choosing CH. The vehicular information, which were considered in this work include Count of vehicles on road side, vehicle distance, transmission range between vehicles, transmission range between vehicle and road side units.

Vehicle's equipment, velocity and location were taken into consideration in the proposed technique for choosing CH. This is performed for improving the stability of cluster and for optimizing available equipment usage in network, particularly, if the operation of the vehicles is towards particular objective. From the vehicles moving in the same direction, CH is chosen. The Virtual Home Environment (VHE) priority factor is indicated with a symbol P. Depending on vehicle's velocity, location and equipment, the election priority factor P of a particular cluster is computed. The below are presumed for processing CH,

- There is a distinct ID number of each vehicle.
- To gather the information of location, direction and velocity regularly, satellite positioning device (GPS) is fitted in each vehicle.
- In each vehicle, instantaneous velocity is indicated as υ in proposed technique.
- Intended vehicle is given as i, in same cluster, vehicle group is indicated as φ_n, vehicle i's group of neighbouring vehicle is specified as φi, and in same cluster, another vehicle is indicated as j. Each vehicle has $N_c - 1$ neighbors, $[j_1, j_2, ..., j_{n-1}]$.

Computation of P is performed as,

Vehicle Equipment Priority: Based on four vehicle classes, vehicle equipment priority factor value P_e, is assumed as like Eq 4.3,

$$P_e = \begin{bmatrix} 3 \text{ for vehicles type V} \\ 2 \text{ for vehicles type } V_s \\ 1 \text{ for vehicles type } V_m \\ 0 \text{ for vehicles type } V_{ms} \end{bmatrix} \quad (4.3)$$

Vehicles equipment priority in one cluster is computed using Eq 4.4,

$$P_{el} = [P_{e1}, P_{e2}, P_{e3}, \dots, P_{eNc}] \quad (4.4)$$

By scaling these values between 0 to 1, they are normalized using Eq 4.5,

$$P_{enorm} = \frac{P_e(i) - \min(P_{el})}{\max(P_{el}) - \min(P_{el})} \; \forall i \in \varphi_n \quad (4.5)$$

Highest equipment priority is assigned to a vehicle having least value of P_{enorm}.

Location Priority: Distances between i and j is computed using Eq 4.6,

$$D_{ij} = \sqrt{(x_i - x_j)^2 + (y_i - y_j)^2} \; \forall j \in \varphi_i \quad (4.6)$$

Every vehicle $(N_c - 1)$ is having distance values (D_{ij}), and vehicle (i)'s summation of all (D_{ij}) values is computed using Eq 4.7,

$$S_d = \sum_{j=1}^{N_c-1} D_{ij} \tag{4.7}$$

Here S_d depicts the summation of distances. Vehicle having smallest S_d is very near to all other vehicles. In the election of CH location priority, highest priority is assigned to this vehicle. It is not required to be at the centre, but it is near to others. Election is depends on location and other parameters and it is not required to elected as CH. Another parameter used is location priority factor P_l, in addition to velocity priority, ID priority and equipment priority which are the additional priority measures for computing certain vehicle's over-all priority. Vehicle's location priority deviation is represented using P1 value based on low S_d vehicle. In order to compute P_l, following Eq 4.8 and Eq 4.9 are used.

$$S_\mu = \min\,[S_d(1), S_d(2), S_d(3), \ldots, S_d(N_c)] \tag{4.8}$$

$$P_{l1} = S_d(i) - s_\mu \quad \forall i \in \varphi_n \tag{4.9}$$

Where $S_\mu \rightarrow$ minimum value of distances

Vehicle's location priority in one cluster is computed using Eq 4.10,

$$P_{lj} = [P_{l1} P_{l2} P_{l3} \ \ldots \ P_{lNc}] \tag{4.10}$$

By scaling these value between 0 to 1, these values are normalized using Eq 4.11,

$$P_{lnorm} = \frac{P_l(i) - \min(P_{l1})}{\max(P_{l1}) - \min(P_{l1})} \quad \forall i \in \varphi_n \tag{4.11}$$

Vehicle having less S_d, $P_{lnorm} = 0$.

Vehicle Velocity Priority: Vehicles instantaneous velocities are assumed as υ_1, υ_2, υ_3 ... υ_n and at time instant t, mean velocity is represented as υ_μ. For every vehicle, P_υ is computed using Eq 4.12,

$$P_v = \frac{1}{n}\left(v(i) - v_{\mu}\right) \forall i \in \varphi_n \quad (4.12)$$

Vehicle's velocity priority in one cluster is computed using Eq 4.13,

$$P_{vl} = [P_{v1} P_{v2} P_{v3} \ \ldots \ P_{vNc}] \quad (4.13)$$

By scaling these value between 0 to 1, these values are normalized using Eq 4.14,

$$P_{vnorm} = \frac{P_v(i) - \min(P_{vI})}{\max(P_{vI}) - \min(P_{vI})} \ \forall i \in \varphi_n \quad (4.14)$$

Highest velocity priority is assigned to a vehicle having lowest $P_{\upsilon norm}$.

Overall Election Priority: Overall priority is computed as function of P_e, P_l and P_υ as like Eq 4.15:

$$P = \frac{1}{w1} P_e + \frac{1}{w2} P_l + \frac{1}{w3} P_v \quad (4.15)$$

Priority factor's weight is computed using weighting values w_1, w_2 and w_3, where $w_1 + w_2 + w_3 = 1$. Vehicle's overall priority in one cluster is computed using Eq 4.16,

$$P_I = [P_1, P_2, P_3, \ldots, P_{Nc}] \quad (4.16)$$

By scaling these value between 0 to 1, these values are normalized using Eq 4.17,

$$P_{norm} = \frac{P(i) - \min(P_I)}{\max(P_I) - \min(P_I)} \ \forall i \in \varphi_n \quad (4.17)$$

In intra cluster communication of a network, to render a robust service, w_1 has huge significance, therefore, it is provided with higher value. Next weight is designated to location (w_2), since vehicle with good location has a better probability of serving others in minimum hop count. End-to-end delay is decreased due to this.

The process of CHE is as below:

1. A HELLO (msg, hop-cnt) message is sent regularly by each user. At the same movement, HELLO messages is relayed to the remaining vehicles also. On M hops, the information of all other vehicles are processed by this vehicle. Hop count (hop-cnt), velocity (υ), location information, cluster election priority P and ID number are included in that information. Information of other vehicle are saved once HELLO message of other vehicles is received. The hop count M of every vehicle is computed with this information, which is stored for future use. The hop count of other vehicles is computed by receiving vehicle while collecting information. The actual M is stored and count is raised by one and this information is then forwarded to next vehicle. M hop of this vehicle is computed by the next vehicle using this procedure. The vehicle has all the information about neighbors vehicle after several transmissions.

2. P(i) is computed by every vehicle (i), after collecting information and results are compared with P(j), if,

$$P(i) < P(j) \ \forall i \in \varphi_n \tag{4.18}$$

High priority is given to a vehicle having low P values. This is done to make this vehicle to update it as CH. If two or more vehicles having less P value which is represented as Eq 4.19

$$\begin{cases} P(i) = P(j) \\ P_e(i) < P_e(j) \end{cases} \tag{4.19}$$

Selected a vehicle having less value of P_e as CH, if,

$$\begin{cases} P_e(i) = P_e(j) \\ ID(i) < ID(j) \end{cases} \tag{4.20}$$

The CH is selected from a vehicle having less ID.

3. After upgrading as a CH, vehicle broadcast a propagating cluster information, HEAD (Cluster ID, head-msg, way-car, hop-cnt) message to outside. Where, cluster label is represented as CluID (Cluster ID), CH vehicle

information is represented as head-msg, route information is represented as way-car and number of hops is represented as hop-cnt. At initial transmission, zero value is assigned to hop-cnt and way-car. After the reception of HEAD message, all values are stored by other vehicles in the cluster and hop-cnt value is examined by it. They will add one to hop-cnt value, if it is less than Mmax and this information is forwarded to next hop. If Mmax is equal to hop-cnt, further treatments are not done. While receiving same CluID, other vehicles investigate about value of M and low value of M is selected for finding their hop-cnt return value. If they receive a message of various CluID, CHs head-msg is analysed by it and retained information of vehicle having highest priority. When hop-cnt is one, CluID is examined by vehicles during HELLO message exchange. If it founds different CluID, then these two vehicles are said to be border nodes.

4. Vehicle selected based on step 2, sends a apply message APPLY (CluID, msg, way-car, hop-cnt) to t CH. This message is interpreted by other vehicles in the route and information about them are added to way-car and hop-cnt is increased by one, then forward it to CH.

5. A vehicle will be added into member list of CH, if vehicles count is less than Nmax. If a vehicle is accepted, it is send with accept message (ACCP), else refuse message (RFUS) is send to it, by CH. Until reaching the vehicle count less than Nmax or joining another cluster, temporary connection is established by a node which is receiving refuse message (RFUS) for accessing resources of a network.

6. The MEMR (CluID, msg, way-car, dis-cnt, hop-cnt) message is broadcasted by intended vehicle, after the reception of ACCP message and then, there is no need of involving in process of other clustering election process via sending dis-cnt to other CHs.

7. Until making all vehicles as member or head of cluster, this process is repeated.

8. Hop-cnt and CluId information is used for searching other cluster's adjacent vehicles by border cluster members and makes a neighbor nodes list.

9. BUND (msg, way-car, dis-cnt, hop-cnt) message hop-cnt is send to CH for indicating that it becomes a boundary vehicle.

10. Vehicle nears to boundary are contacted by a vehicle having RFUS message and until constructing new cluster using other vehicles or finding new CH, temporary connection is established with this vehicle.

4.3.3 Cluster Formation

Clustering in vehicular ad hoc networks (VANET) is one of the control techniques for dynamic topology. Several VANET clustering algorithms are obtained from mobile adhoc networks (MANET). But, VANET nodes are qualified by their high mobility, and the presence of VANET nodes in the same geographic vicinity does not imply that they show the same mobility patterns. Hence, the clustering approaches of VANET must take the speed and velocity of nodes into consideration to build a stable clustering form. The vehicles and Roadside unit are taken as nodes in the VANET. The vehicles move with different speeds. The vehicles of a VANET are fitted with the DRSC (Dedicated Short Range Communication). the positions of vehicle are given by the GPS. In the discussed algorithm the vehicles moving in the same direction are regarded as neighbours. Vehicles can move along the same road way and transceiver information. Communication from the source node can either directly get to the destination or via an intermediate node that may be a router or a road side unit. In vehicle to vehicle communication (V2V), vehicles are supported in a common range to be able to communicate among themselves. However, in vehicle to roadside (V2R) vehicles communicate via access points on the network that results in much overhead and delay.

From the CH table available of a non-CH node, which has stopped its timer chooses the closest node in the form of cluster head once the head selection period is done. A JOIN message is sent by this node to a elected head in the form of an acknowledgement and in the next round, this node will become a member of CH. In this, the size of cluster is limited, however the number of members in cluster is not limited in cluster creation. For covering the cluster, two clusters with the same area needs same number of active vehicles on an average, owing to vehicles being activated. Around the heads of clusters, Voronoi-shaped clusters are formed due to the closest CH selection.

4.4 CLUSTER MESSAGE REPLICATION QUOTA DECISION MAKING

For the faster and successful communication to make faster decision regarding traffic information, in this work messages are replicated. To reduce the communication overhead, in this work replication messages are limited based nodes count within cluster. Assume there is L copies of messages which needs to be propagated. Propagation of these copies must be initiated at the same movement they are created. When compared with RU-DCN, tree based distribution depends replication method is used here for achieving the same.

- For a message M, propagation quota or load L is set by source node;
- Upon encountering another node, propagation load L is distributed by source node, so that, load L is split as two halves (or $L - \lfloor L/2 \rfloor$ and $\lfloor L/2 \rfloor$);

- After t time steps, consider encounter between receiver node n_j, which does not processed any message M and messenger node ni with message M, having q_t quota value. The replication process distribution is done, so that, nodes n_i and n_j will have $q_{i,t}$ replications of t messages while node n_j will be given $q_{j,t}$ replications, where $q_{j,t} = \lfloor q_{t2} \rfloor$ and $q_{i,t} = q_t - q_{j,t}$;
- Until stabilising the value of qt as 1 for a finite time steps count, this process is continued. At this point, carrier node corresponds to messenger node and further distribution is not performed;
- If carrier node's speed is less than encountering node's relative speed, message will not be carried to encountering node by carrier node.

4.5 RESULTS AND DISCUSSION

Experimentation is done using 64 -bit Ubuntu 12.04 operating system having Intel Core i7-2670QM processor @ 2.20 GHz and RAM of 8 GB. The network simulator tool used is NS2.34. The performance of the hybrid algorithm is analyzed by conducting various experiments. Due to stochastic quality of optimization algorithm, the algorithm is executed ten times and the result is analyzed with the average value. Table 4.2 provides simulation software parameters.

Table 4.2 Simulation software parameters

PRODUCTS	QUANTITY
Number of Vehicles	100 – 150
Dimension of simulation area	1000 X 1300 sq. meters
Simulation Time	150s
Physical layer Protocol	802.11p

Packet size	256 bytes
Data rate	4 Mbps
Number of lanes	2
Vehicle velocity	20-60 kmph
Number of Iteration	70

4.5.1 Simulation Results

Figures 4.3 – 4.6 illustrates the performance analysis of proposed technique with respect to average throughput, routing overhead, delay and packet delivery ratio.

In the following Table 4.3, packet delivery ratio values obtained for the proposed and existing research techniques has been shown.

Table 4.3 Packet delivery ratio values

Number of vehicles	Methods		
	FCD-TSM	3 Stage fuzzy decision tree model	EcoTrec
100	62.4	53.3	49.2
110	69.88	56.4	53.7
120	73.67	69.6	62.9
130	75.3	72.5	67.6
140	76.5	74.1	71.3
150	82.7	79.55	73.2

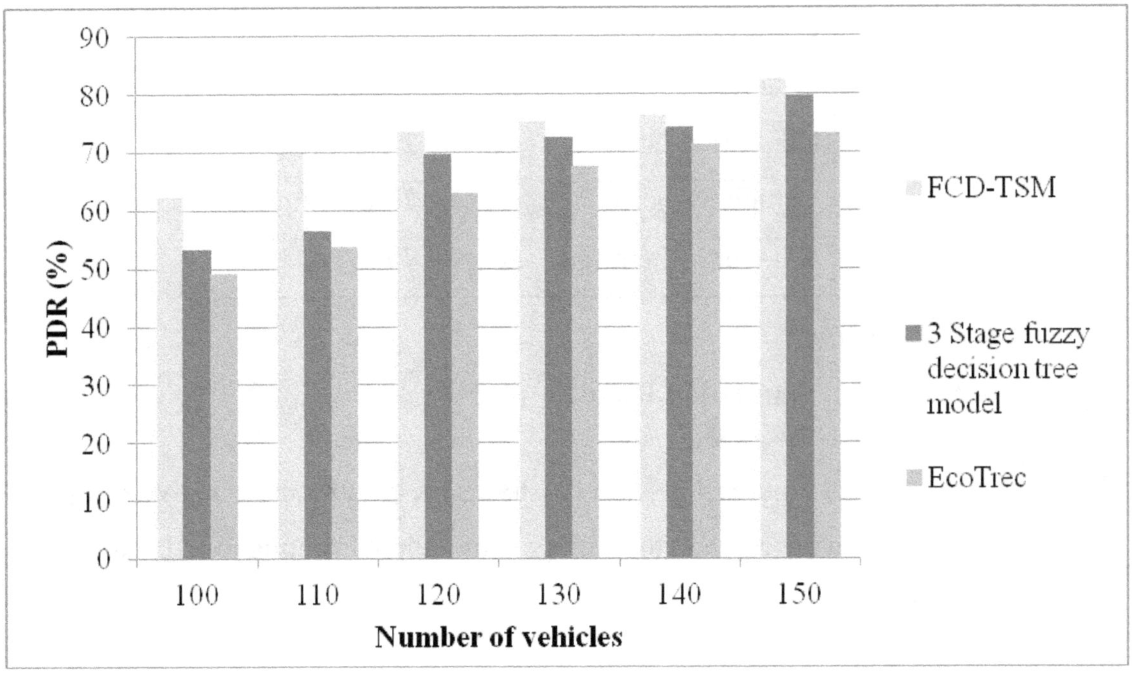

Figure 4.3 Packet Delivery Ratio Vs Number of vehicles

The vehicle count influence on packet delivery ratio was shown in Figure 4.3. PDR is a ratio of packets count sent to packets count received. When vehicles count increases, PDR also increases. Plot clearly illustrates that the PDR is higher in FCD-TSM approach compared to the other techniques. From the graphical comparison it is confirmed that the proposed method FCD-TSM shows 8.63% increased packet delivery ratio than 3 Stage fuzzy decision tree model and 16.55% increased packet delivery ration than EcoTrec.

In the following Table 4.4, routing overhead values obtained for the proposed and existing research techniques has been shown.

Table 4.4 Routing Overhead values

Number of vehicles	Methods		
	FCD-TSM	3 Stage fuzzy decision tree model	EcoTrec
100	22.4	23.3	25.6
110	29.88	26.4	27.9
120	27.67	39.6	42.4
130	35.3	42.9	45.6
140	46.5	49.4	53.2
150	48.7	52.52	55.4

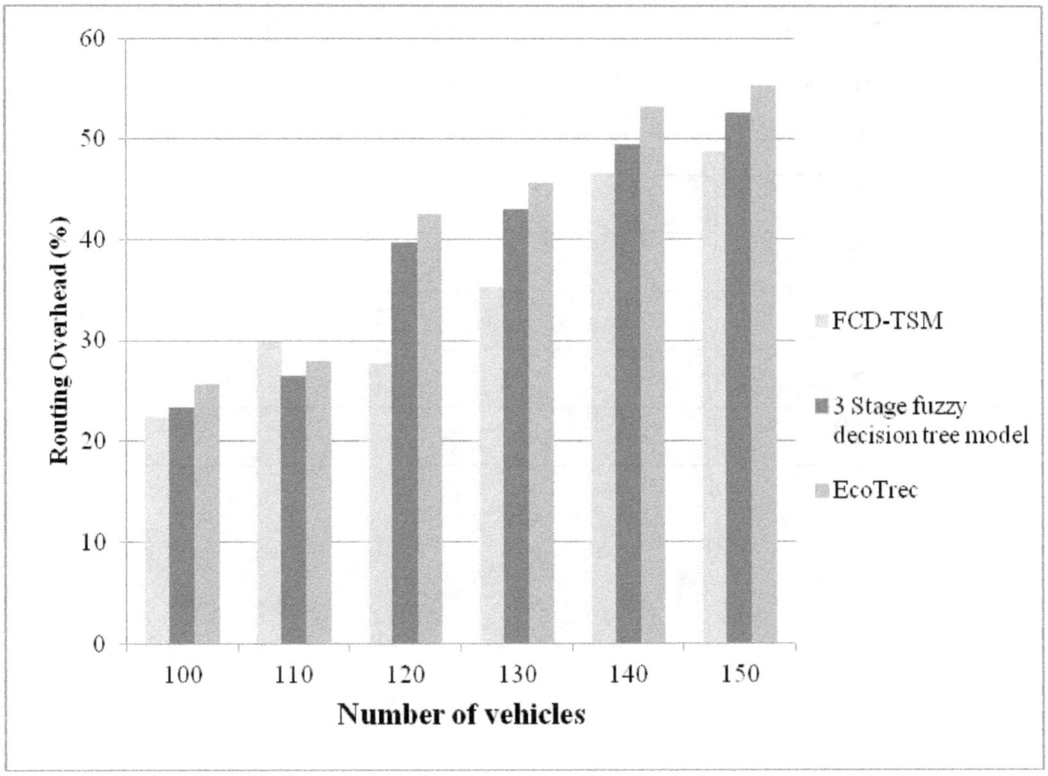

Figure 4.4 Routing overhead Vs Number of vehicles

The influence of the number of vehicles and the routing overhead was shown in Figure 4.4. Packets count distributed per data packet specifies routing overhead. When vehicles count increases there will be an increase in routing overhead. The packet loss is comparatively lesser in the FCD-TSM technique. From this comparison it is confirmed that the proposed FCD-TSM shows 10.11% reduced routing overhead than 3 stage fuzzy decision tree model and 15.85% reduced routing overhead than EcoTrec.

In the following Table 4.5, delay values obtained for the proposed and existing research techniques has been shown.

Table 4.5 Delay values

Number of vehicles	Methods		
	FCD-TSM	**3 Stage fuzzy decision tree model**	**EcoTrec**
100	15	18	22
110	15.5	21	23
120	17	24	27
130	18	25	29
140	21	27	31
150	23	29	35

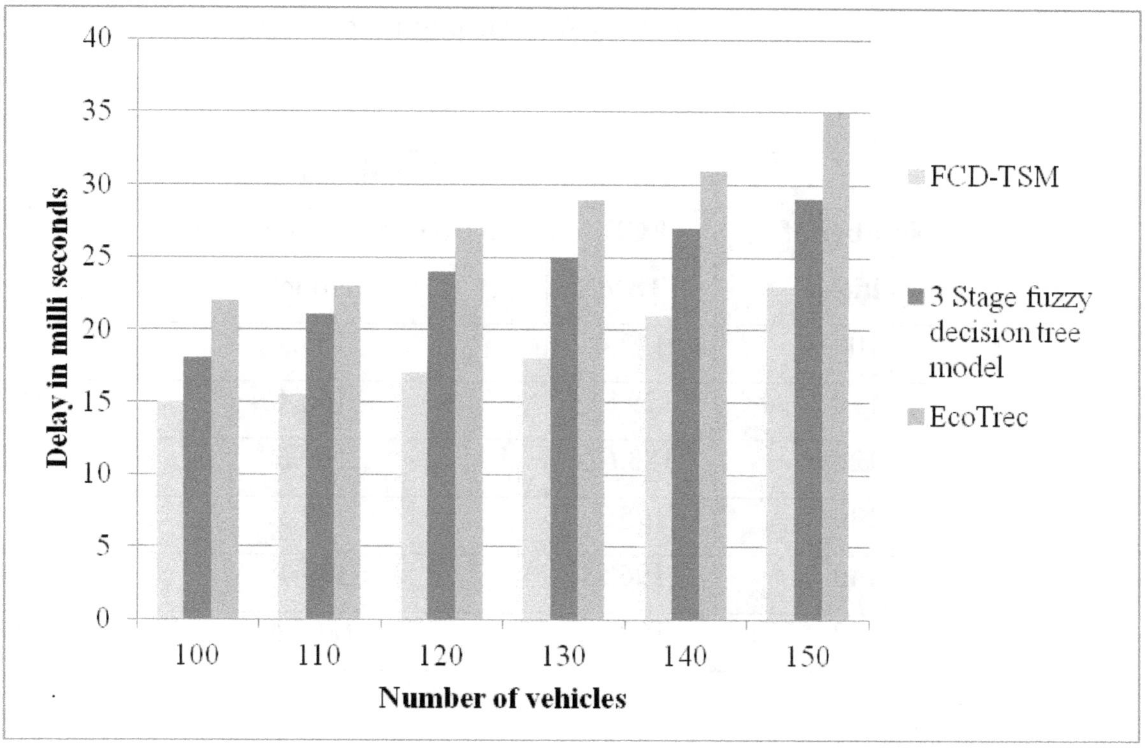

Figure 4.5 Delay values

The vehicle counts impact and delay was shown in Figure 4.5. From this figure it is proved that the proposed methods tends to have better outcome with lesser delay which is considerably better than the existing work 3 Stage fuzzy decision tree model. From this comparison it is proved that the proposed method FCD-TSM shows 23.95% lesser delay than 3 stage fuzzy decision tree model and 34.43% lesser delay in EcoTrec.

In the following Table 4.6, throughput values obtained for the proposed and existing research techniques has been shown.

Table 4.6 Throughput values

Number of vehicles	Methods		
	FCD-TSM	3 Stage fuzzy decision tree model	EcoTrec
100	172.4	153.3	149.2
110	179.81	166.4	155.4
120	183.67	169.6	161.7
130	195.3	172.5	164.8
140	196.5	179.1	171.5
150	192.7	180.56	174.7

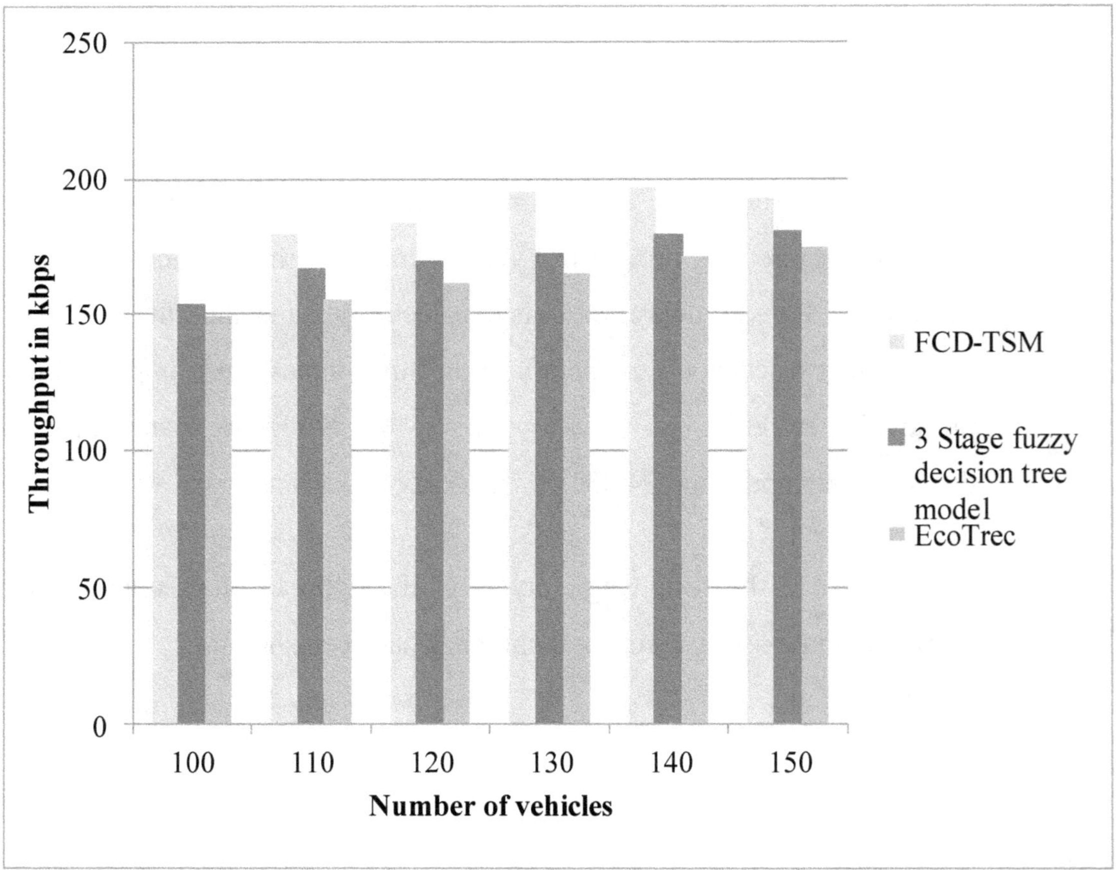

Figure 4.6 Average Throughput Vs Number of vehicles

The vehicle counts impact and average throughput was shown in Figure 4.6. The number of successful reception of packets defines throughput. Packet delivery rate is increased relatively in the proposed technique. It is observed that the average throughput is more in TCD-TSM technique. From this comparison it is confirmed that the proposed FCD-TSM shows 9.68% higher throughput than 3 stage fuzzy decision tree model and 14.64% higher throughput than EcoTrec.

4.6 CONCLUSION

In practical vehicular adhoc network environment, reducing fuel consumption is a major challenge that is highlighted in this technical work. In this work, reducing fuel consumption is ensured by reducing the waiting time of vehicles in the road traffic by taking accurate and rapid decision on managing the traffic. This is accomplished by presenting the technique, which is named as Fuel Consumption and Delay aware Traffic Scheduling Method (FCD-TSM). To support the vehicles with various ranges of transmission and sensitivity in this research work, coverage aware clustering is performed in which VANET nodes will be classified together through which quicker data communication can be guaranteed. To make sure that the data transmission is successful and decision making is accurate, in this research work message replication quota is determined based on the nodes count in cluster, which decrease the network load and guarantee that the data transmission is successful. MATLAB environment is used for evaluating this technical work and the proposed work shows improved results in comparison with available work as depicted by experimentation results. It is ensured from the graphical comparison that the proposed technique FCD-TSM depcits 8.63% improved packet delivery ratio compared to 3 Stage fuzzy decision tree model and 16.55% improved packet delivery ration compared to EcoTrec. FCD-TSM reveals 10.11% decreased routing overhead compared to 3 stage fuzzy decision tree model and 15.85% decreased routing overhead compared to EcoTrec. FCD-TSM reveals 23.95% reduced delay compared to 3 stage fuzzy decision tree model and 34.43% reduced delay in EcoTrec. FCD-TSM exhibits 9.68% better throughput compared 3 stage fuzzy decision tree model and 14.64% improved throughput compared EcoTrec. In future scenario, more practical traffic information must be considered for the accurate decision making. Artificial intelligence approaches and the optimization methods can be presented for the accurate and rapid decision making.

CHAPTER 5

FUEL CONSUMPTION AND COVERAGE AWARE DYNAMIC ROUTING IN VANET

5.1 INTRODUCTION

Vehicular ad-hoc networks are a subcategory of mobile ad-hoc networks that render a unique mechanism for smart transport systems. Vehicular ad-hoc networks are wireless networks that yield features including safety and comfort of the driver (Hamdi *et al.* 2020). In VANET the vehicles indicate the nodes of a network and these nodes are travelling at extremely high speed in an urban region. It is an independent and self-configuring wireless communication network. Since mobile wireless devices and networks have gained considerable importance, the need for Vehicle-to-Vehicle (V2V) and Vehicle-to Roadside (VRC) or Vehicle-to-Infrastructure (V2I) Communication will constantly rise. VANETs can be used for an extensive range of safety and non-safety applications, permit for value added services like vehicle safety, automated toll payment, traffic management, improved navigation, location-based services including finding the nearest fuel station, restaurant or travel lodge and infotainment applications like giving access to the Internet. In the past few years, several research attempts have been made, which have examined different problems associated with V2I, V2V, and VRC areas due to the critical role they are anticipated to play in Intelligent Transportation Systems (ITSs). In practice, different VANET projects have been undertaken by different governments, industries, and academic organizations worldwide in the past decade or so (Dhawan & Nagpal 2016).

In smart transportation systems, every vehicle has the role of sender, receiver, and router for broadcasting information to the vehicular network or transportation agency, which later utilizes the information that safe, an independent trafficflow is ensured. In order to have communications happen between vehicles and Road Side Units (RSUs), vehicles should be fitted with some kind of radio interface or On Board Unit (OBU), which facilitates short-range wireless ad hoc networks that has to be established (Wang *et al.* 2017). Vehicles should also be installed with hardware, which allows extensive position information including Global Positioning System (GPS) or a Differential Global Positioning System (DGPS) receiver. Fixed RSUs, connected to the backbone network, should be present to enable communication. The number and distribution of roadside units is based on the communication protocol, which must be utilized. For instance, few protocols need roadside units to be distributed uniformly all through the entire road networks; few need roadside units just at intersections, whereas others need roadside units just at region borders. Eventhough it is safer to presume that infrastructure is present to some level and vehicles should have intermittent access to it, it is impractical to expect that vehicles can access roadside units through wireless (Wang *et al.* 2017).

VANETs are a specific branch of MANETs. Owing to the rapid movement of the vehicles, their topology is more quickly and dynamically varying in comparison with MANETs. However, the mobility of the vehicular nodes is limited by present roads infrastructure. Speed limits, congestion level, and traffic control systems such as traffic lights and stop symbols also impose a limitation on the vehicular node velocities. In addition, future vehicular nodes can be empowered with bigger transmission ranges, extended on board storage and sensing potential, and rechargeable energy sources. Dissimilar to MANETs, VANETs are abundant in storage and processing power abilities that improves their flexibility and compatibility of performing computationally complex tasks.

There are different technical problems encountered while designing effective vehicular communications. One of the most crucial problems of the vehicular ad hoc network is to design a scalable and robust multi-hop routing protocol, which has the capability of rendering an optimum route for forwarding the packets to the destination (Abbasi *et al.* 2018). Ensuring a stable, reliable, optimal, and trustworthy multi-hop routing strategy over VANETs is a basic move towards implementing effective vehicular ad hoc communications. Several evolving applications in vehicular communication need the help of multi-hop communications. One of them includes on board active safety approaches that is very useful to drivers to prevent ramming and yield coordinated operation at critical locations such as highway entries and city intersection/junctions. Using safety system information on roads such as real-time traffic congestion, traffic accidents, road surface conditions, or high-speed levy can be intelligently distributed. By this, the road congestion can be avoided. It also massively decreases the vehicle accidents and can save several valuable lives. Also, inter-vehicular communication can render entertainment and infotainment applications. These include information on weather conditions, positions of gas stations and restaurants, e-commerce, and infotainment applications such as accessing the internet, downloading music, and content delivery (Zhou *et al.* 2017).

The features such as uneven distribution of vehicles on the road, massive sized network, extreme mobility owing to the high speed of the vehicles, often varying topology, and interference to communication owing to obstacle disturbance increase the challenges for routing the data in the vehicular ad hoc network (Ming *et al.* 2018). A major number of the available routing approaches do not have the capability of determining the optimal routes since they are inefficient in including the above stated features of VANETs. One of the issues with these routing protocols is that they frequently forward the packet towards destination taking those streets, whose vehicular density is not high. Consequently, the packet satisfies a local optimum condition. Local optimum is a condition when a forwarding node is not able to find the adjacent neighbour due to the absence of traffic density on the street. The node maintains the packet in its buffer for a longer amount of time. In case a packet is present in the buffer for a longer time, it's time to live field runs out and is later ignored. This deteriorates the network performance in terms of end-to-end delay and packet delivery ratio. Developing a routing protocol having the capability of resolving such problems is crucial and the discussed protocol tries to get over this problem by choosing several connected streets having higher vehicular density depending on several intersections.

The important objective of this technical work is to present the approaches that can carry out optimal routing in the VANET environment considering the challenges of coverage and load over the network. This technical work is primarily highlighted on decreasing the fuel usage that might happen because of the heavy traffic experienced on the road side. The proposed research approach is discussed in detail in the sub sections that follows.

5.2 INFORMATION GATHERING FROM ROAD SIDE UNITS

At first, the traffic information on the vehicles in the road is gathered to take a right decision on vehicle routing. This traffic information is collected with the objective of improving the routing decision making, and this way a substantial reduction in fuel consumption usage can be attained. In this research work, static road side units are taken into account for collecting the information. This RSU will be static within the transmission range of vehicles, and hence the road side information can be gathered. Every RSU installed on the road sides will gather the data by transmitting polling, and request messages. In this, first the RSU will do a broadcast of the polling messages. In case the node is present then the request message will be transmitted for the data gathering. Depending on request message, reply message will be transmitted back with the necessary traffic information. The overview of the information collection process from the road side units are discussed in detail in the earlier chapter under section 4.2.

5.3 CLUSTER HEAD SELECTION USING FUZZY ANT COLONY ALGORITHM

Once data is collected from the road side units, cluster head selection is carried out among the vehicles spread in the region. This is performed to streamline the data transmission process, thereby rapid and robust data communication can be ensured. In this research work, optimal cluster head selection is carried out by using the fuzzy ant colony algorithm. Ant colony optimization (ACO) is a strong optimization approach, which has been used for resolving several complex optimization problems. The merits of ant colony algorithm is listed below: 1. Inherent parallelism 2. Positive Feedback accounts for rapid discovery of good solutions 3. Efficient for Traveling Salesman Problem and similar problems. One such optimization challenge involves cluster head selection in the vehicular adhoc network environment. This problem need concurrent optimization of several goals, including monetary expense, average network delay, hop count between communicating nodes, and reliability under a bunch of conditions. This research work introduces a multi-objective ant colony optimization algorithm for solving the VANET cluster head selection problem with efficiency by including the fuzzy logic in the ACO algorithm.

5.3.1 Ant Colony Optimization

The ACO algorithm is influenced by the collaborative behavior of ants. Pheromone is released by an ant when it travels through a path. During the process of path discovery, ants get attracted by pheromone to go along the links having the biggest pheromone concentrations. With the passage of time, shortest paths will be more often visited and pheromone will be accumulated quicker on them, which in turn results in more ants to choose these paths. This way, the pheromone deposits renders a favourable feedback to ants by re-emphasizing on good selections. In the case of ACO, the optimization problem is devised as a graph. Ants simultaneously and asynchronously move through the neighbouring states of the problem by constructing paths on the graph. Through movement, ants iteratively build solutions for the optimization problem. The movement of an ant is ruled by a stochastic local decision policy, which uses pheromone trails and heuristic information. At every step of the solution construction, ant *k* builds the next node utilizing a probabilistic action selection rule, which governs the probability with which ant *k* will select to move from current node i to next node j:

$$p_{ij}^{k}(t) = \frac{[T_{ij}(t)]^{\alpha_{ant}}[\eta_{ij}]^{\beta_{ant}}}{\sum_{l\in N_i}[T_{il}(t)]^{\alpha_{ant}}[\eta_{il}]^{\beta_{ant}}} \tag{5.1}$$

where N_i refers to the set of links l present at decision node i, $p_{ij}^{k}(t)$, stands for the probability of choosing a link between nodes i and j for the k^{th}ant, τ_{ij} indicates the pheromone on link between i and j, and η_{ij} specifies the heuristic value of link between i and j. α_{ant} and βant indicates the effect of pheromone

(5.2)

content and heuristic correspondingly. After every iteration t of the algorithm (that is, when all ants have finished a solution) trails are updated with

$$\tau_{ij}(t) = \varrho . \tau_{ij}(t-1) + \Delta_{\tau_{ij}}$$

where ϱ refers to a user-specified evaporation/forgetting constant, and $\Delta_{\tau_{ij}}$ indicates the sum of the contributions made by all ants, which are utilized to change 'ij' to build their solution. The contributions made by ants are in proportion to the quality of the attained solutions. It implies that the better the solution produced by an ant, the greater will be the trail contribution included to the moves it utilized.

5.3.2 Fuzzy Logic

Various techniques for dealing with the multi-objective factors by getting a Pareto set of solutions have been published in literature. Recently, fuzzy logic has also achieved considerable focus for MOO problems, finding applications in several fields, including analog circuit design, war resource allocation, direct current electromagnet design, and facility location selection. The principle of fuzzy logic depends on a multi valued logic in which a statement could be partially true and partially false simultaneously. A fuzzy logic approach is different from binary logic, the aspect being that binary logic lets a statement to be have either false or true value. The binary logic scheme performs the mathematical mapping to a concise set X, where every element x $\in$X can either fall under a set or not. Contradictory to binary logic, fuzzy logic defines an approximate truth value of a proposition that depends on linguistic variables and inference rules. Therefore, in fuzzy sets, an element may partly be a member of a set. This partial membership is defined using a membership function, μ, lying in the range [0,1], where μ is utilized for deciding the degree of membership to the fuzzy set. A linguistic variable is a variable whose values are words or sentences expressed in natural or artificial language. A specialist can create rules suing linguistic variables, with edges, for instance, 'more', 'many', 'few', and connectors including AND, OR, and NOT. These rules will be utilized by an inference engine to enable close reasoning.

Similar to crisp sets, set operations including intersection, union, and the complement, are also specified on fuzzy sets. Zadeh initially recommended the implementation of the 'AND' and the 'OR' in the form of 'min' and 'max' operations. But, in particular multi-objective applications, Zadeh's 'AND' and 'OR' operators are found to be have good rigidity. In the last few years, several modifications have been introduced for Zadeh's operators. Few modifications rendered probability operators, bounded operators, Einstein's operators, Hamacher's operators, ordered weighted average (OWA) operator, and the unified AND-OR (UAO) operator. The OWA operator has been used for several MOO problems. The concept behind designing OWA was that MOO problems usually contain two extreme techniques in establishing a single objective function out of sub-objective functions. In the first case, all the objectives must be met, which results in the pure-ANDing operation. At the other hand, any one of the objectives can be met, thus implying the pure-ORing operation. But, for several real world problems, it is not necessary to derive multi-objective decision functions with pure "ANDing" of t-norm operators nor the pure "ORing" of s-norm operators. The reason behind this is the full deficit of compensation of t-norm operators for any kind of partial satisfaction and full submission of s-norm operators to fulfill any sub-objective. This inference resulted in designing the Ordered Weighted Averaging (OWA) operator.

The UAO operator is a small changed version of the OWA operator. The primary difference between the two operators is that the OWA has two individual equations for representing the AND and the OR functions.

But, UAO utilizes a single equation, still the operator has the capability of acting either as the OWAAND or the OWA-OR operator. The behavior is managed by a variable $v \geq 0$, whose value determines if the function will act as AND or OR. The operator is expressed as

$$f(a,b) = \frac{ab+v\max\{a,b\}}{v+\max\{a,b\}} = \begin{cases} I_* = \mu_{A\cup B}(x) \text{ if } v > 1 \\ I^* = \mu_{A\cap B}(x) \text{ if } V < 1 \end{cases} \quad (5.3)$$

where a indicates the membership value of μ_A(i.e. a = μ_A), b stands for the membership value of μ_B(i.e. b = μ_B), and f(a, b) refers to the value of the overall objective function (i.e. f(a, b) = μ_{AB}).I^*refers to the AND operation that uses the UAO operator, and I_*stands for the OR operation that uses the UAO operator.

5.3.3 Fuzzy Ant Colony Based Cluster Head Selection

The ACO has a population of ants, in which every ant is accountable for establishing a practical network topology. The ant begins with the root node and then eventually develops a topology. The directing factors in the process of decision and choice of a specific path include the heuristic value, pheromone trail, and evaporation. A whole tour by an ant leads to a full practical network topology. Every step of the proposed fuzzy ACO is given below.

Initialization: As ACO is a population based algorithm, initialization comprises of the generation of a group of solutions. These initial solutions are produced in random. It implies that, every ant generates a solution with no feedback or earlier information on the paths. But, while an ant generates a solution, the constraints are verified at every step to guarantee practical initial solutions. The initialization of the algorithm parameters including pheromone deposit and evaporation rates, and the values of α_{ant} and $\beta_{ant}$are also done in this stage.

Ants Activity: After the generation of the initial set of solutions, the next step is to get the probability of choosing the link l between nodes i and j for the kth ant, and to use the pheromone deposit and pheromone evaporation constraints. The technique used in this work is to update the pheromone values depending on the solution produced by only the "elitist" ant. In each iteration that follows initialization, every ant builds a solution utilizing the link selection probability function. After all the ants have completed their tour and got a valid solution, the ant generating the highest value is considered as the elitist ant. This ant is permitted to have the pheromone value updated. For every link occurring in the solution of the elitist ant, the pheromone is updated by adding $\Delta_{\tau ij}$ to the link's present pheromone concentration. Pheromone evaporation happens on every link, with no regard to the links being a segment of the elitist ant or not. The updated values of pheromone are later sent to the next following ants, and the cycle above is repeated till a predetermined termination condition is satisfied. The primary benefit of the above mentioned elitist ant approach is that the technique makes the ants to search with more strength close to the best solution, which has been found till now. But, the technique is affected by a drawback of having too much exploitation, and less exploration.

Fuzzy Heuristic value: A fuzzy heuristic value is included in Equation (1). The heuristic value η_{ij} fundamentally renders a perspective into the structure of the different elements belonging to the solution. In the context of DLAN topology design, every element is a link between any two nodes i and j. The heuristic value of a link is computed as provided by the rule as follows:

IF a link is *near optimum cost* AND *near optimum depth* AND *near optimum reliability* **THEN** it has *high heuristic value*

The above rule can be mathematically expressed with the help of OWA operator as below:

$$\eta_{ij} = \beta^{e} \times \min\{\mu_1(l_j), \mu_2(l_j), \mu_3(l_j)\} + (1 - \beta^{e}) \times \frac{1}{3}\sum_{i=1}^{3} \mu_i(l_j) \quad (5.4)$$

In Equation (6), η_{ij} refers to the fuzzy set of high heuristic value and β^{e} indicates a constant in the range [0,1]. $\mu_1(l_i)$, $\mu_2(li)$, and $\mu_3(l_i)$ correspondingly indicate the memberships in the fuzzy sets close to the optimum monetary cost, close to the optimum depth, and close to the optimum reliability correspondingly.

The membership of a link with regard to near optimum monetary cost is decided as below. From the cost matrix, which provides the costs of every possible link, the minimum and maximum costs among each of the link costs are computed. These minimum and maximum costs are considered as the lower (LCMin) and upper (LCMax) threshold. Later, the membership of a link is computed with regard to these bounds considering the equation below

$$\mu_1(l_j) = \begin{cases} 1 & \text{if LC} \le \text{LCMin} \\ \frac{\text{LCMax}-\text{LC}}{\text{LCMax}-\text{LCMin}} & \text{if LCMin} < LC < LCMax \\ 0 & \text{if LC} > LCMax \end{cases} \quad (5.5)$$

where "LC" indicates the current cost of the link. The membership function of near optimum depth, μ_2, can be specified in a similar manner. The lower bound, "LDMin", is considered to be a depth of 1 with regard to the root. The upper bound, "LDMax", is considered to be the maximum depth created in the initial solution or a maximum of a user defined threshold. 1 The membership function for near optimum depth is expressed by

$$\mu_2(l_j) = \begin{cases} 1 & \text{if LD} \le \text{LDMin} \\ \frac{\text{LDMax}-\text{LD}}{\text{LDMax}-\text{LDMin}} & \text{if LDMin} < LD \le LDMax \\ 0 & \text{if LD} > LDMax \end{cases} \quad (5.6)$$

where “LD” indicates the current depth of the link with regard to the root node. At last, the membership function for reliability, μ_3, can be decided by getting the maximum (LRMax) and the minimum (LRMin) bounds for the reliability. The membership value for reliability is decided as

$$\mu_3(l_i) = \begin{cases} 1 & \text{if } LR \geq LRMax \\ \frac{LRMax - LR}{LRMax - LRMin} & \text{if } LRMin < LR \leq LRMax \\ 0 & \text{if } LR < LRMin \end{cases} \quad (5.7)$$

where “LR” indicates the current reliability of the link.

5.4 COVERAGE AND LOAD AWARE CLUSTERING

In this research work, coverage and load aware clustering is presented for clustering the vehicles on the basis of the chosen cluster head. The optimal cluster size gives a lower limit of the average energy consumption per unit square. But, this kind of an ideal network positioning may not be the real scenario in real time vehicular networks. Practically, a VANET network is frequently deployed by random distribution of vehicles into a massive but restricted road field. Consider a VANET of N vehicles that are randomly spread in a road. a(n) is used to represent the sensing field of a single vehicle. The network coverage of N vehicles is defined as $\bigcup_{n=1}^{N} a(n)$, and the network coverage ratio is expressed as

$$\rho(N) = \frac{(\bigcup_{n=1}^{N} a(n)) \cap A}{A} \quad (5.8)$$

Depending on this measured value and the load consideration clustering of vehicles will be carried out that will guarantee the rapid data communication, therefore a rapid decision making can be performed.

The objective is to get the best clustering structure $C=\{C_1, C_2,...,C_s\}$ which best meets the network goals in terms of coordination performance and its overhead expenses. Forming the best cluster by exhaustively searching every possible combination of cluster is very complicated particularly if the network size is big. Applications of coalitional game theory in VANET is an evolving principle particularly with coordination of the network generally to decrease this complexity. It yields a scalable analytical model to yield distributed, less overhead, less sophisticated solutions. Coalition game theory is used and a coalition formation game is setup for modelling the dynamic clustering problem for coordination in downlink and a utility function is employed for the joint optimization of SE and LB.

Let N = $\{SC_1, SC_2,...,SC_n\}$ refer to the players of the game, i.e. every player denotes an SC in this scenario. Grand coalition is defined to be the distinct set of all cells in the game, i.e. N itself. Any cluster of SCs within the grand coalition is specified as a coalition $C_i = \{SC_{i1}, SC_{i2,...,}SC_{iz}\}$. A collection is specified as a set of coalitions $C = \{C_1, C_2,....,C_s\}$ and a collection is known as a partition in case all the coalitions within C are disjoint coalitions i.e. $\forall i \neq j, C_i \cap C_j = \phi$and all players (SCs) are added in one of the coalitionsi.e. $\cup_{i=1}^{s} C_i = N$.

The utility (payoff) of a coalition C_i within the partition C is specified as $u(C_i, C)$ and the overall coalition game is distinctly specified by (N,u) pair. Utility of any coalition consists of both the advantage and the cost for coordination. Utility function for collaborative clusters in this scenario considers SE and cell load distribution to be the benefits and uses a cost factor with increased computational complexity, pilot overhead and backhaul requirement with the cluster size increase. The cost factor in the utility avoids a super-additive game, i.e. there is an increase in cost with cluster size and therefore it is generally impractical to obtain all SCs to collaborate in one single cluster. The features form of a coalition game is specified such that the utility of any coalition $u(C_i)$ does not rely on the way the rest of the partition $(N\backslash C_i)$ is organized i.e. $\forall i\ u(C_i, C) = u(C_i)$. In this scenario, as clustering modifications are proposed in longer time intervals (seconds, minutes) where rapid fading variations are averaged out as defined in (6), the amount of interference generated from the cells external to the cluster include the same irrespective of their clustering form.

For comparing the choice between 2 collections $C=\{C_1, C_2,...,C_s\}$ and $H = \{H_1, H_2,...H_b\}$ of the same subset of players P where $P \subseteq N$, a comparison relation F is defined, where C F H implies that coalitions in C is chosen over the coalitions in H. Different comparison orders but two orders have primary significance for coalitional games for coordinative wireless networks. The first one includes the utilitarian order which provides the comparison between the utility of the overall collection. The players in P choose to shift to collection C from collection H i.e. $C \rhd H$ if $\sum_{i=1}^{s} u(C_i) > \sum_{i=1}^{b} u(H_i)$, otherwise said, the total utility of all the coalitions within collection C is more than the one present in collection H, regardless of the various player utilities. The second significant order is called as pareto order which provides a comparison between the different player utilities to ensure that none of the players get worse owing to the formation of new collection and at least one player is good. For a certain subset of players P, the utility of player P_i in collection C is represented as $u(P_i, C)$; then $C \rhd H$ if $\forall i \in P, u(P_i, C) \geq u(P_i, H)$.

It's extremely desirable to use utilitarian order in the coalition game to increase the system utility on the whole. The objective of the discussed coalition formation game is to increase the overall utility irrespective of the utility for any separate SC. Otherwise said, in case the utility gain of a set of SCs is more compared to the utility loss of the rest of the

SCs, then the respective clustering modification shall be carried out. In a common hotspot scenario, cluster modifications work towards reducing the load for SCs having extremely high load (players having a better payoff) but this will invariably result in the traffic to increase in other SC where the load is not as much (players exhibiting the worse payoff). This change in clustering is desirable in utilitarian order in case there is an increase in overall utility, but this is not permitted in pareto order since few players are worse off irrespective of the overall utility. To create coalitions and dynamically use the coalitions depending on user profile/network modifications, 2 easy transformation rules are adopted:

Merge: Players (SCs) in any two or more coalitions $\{C_1, C_{2,...,}C_s\}$ choose to combine into one coalition $F = \cup_{i=1}^{s} C_i \text{ i.e.}, \cup_{i=1}^{s} C_i \rhd \{C_1, C_2, \ldots, C_s\}, \text{if } u(F) > (\sum_{i=1}^{s} u(C_i))$adoptng the utiliterian order.

Split: Players (SCs) choose to divide from any coalition C_i into smaller coalitions $\{C_{i1}, C_{i2}, \ldots, C_{iy}\}$ where $C_i = \cup_{j=1}^{y} C_{ij} \text{ i.e.}, \{C_{i1}, C_{i2}, \ldots, C_{iy}\} \rhd C_i \text{if} \left(\sum_{j=1}^{y} u(C_{ij}) > u(C_i)\right)$ adopting utiliterian order.

5.4.1 Merge And Split Operation

Let C = $\{C_1, C_2, \ldots, C_s\}$ refer to a partition of N, i.e. the present status of the network. It is expected to begin the merge operation with C_i that has achieved the maximum absolute payoff value. In both utility functions, high absolute payoff value indicates coalitions having the highest number of active users and therefore high load. Coalition C_i searches for neighbour coalitions C_j for any merge operation possible. Neighbour coalition concept is defined to prevent exhaustive search performed for merge operation and decrease the complexity, i.e. merge operation will not be attempted for all the other coalitions in the system but solely towards the neighbourhood coalitions.

Neighbor definitions are carried out by using the average received reference signal level measurements obtained from the users. In the first step, a simple neighbor relations list is carried out at SC level. For any UE_k in the serving region of SC_m, the average received signal from all other SC_j where $P_{kj}^{rx} > P_{min}^{nei}$ are compared. A neighbor rank count is then incremented for $\{SC_m, SC_j\}$ pair if $\frac{P_{kj}^{rx}}{P_{km}^{rx}} > P_{\Delta}^{nei}$. After every SC includes a rank based neighbor list, then neighbors at cluster level are computed similarly i.e. the neighbor rank is incremented for $\{C_m, C_j\}$ coalition pair when $SC_m \subseteq C_m$, $SC_j \subseteq C_j$, $\frac{P_{kj}^{rx}}{P_{km}^{rx}} > P_{\Delta}^{nei}$ and $P_{kj}^{rx} > P_{min}^{nei}$. The probability of a merge operation is verified for all neighbor coalitions of coalition C_i and merge is carried out with C_j if $u(C_i \cup C_j) > u(C_i) + u(C_j)$ on the basis of utilitarian order.

After a successful merge operation, the neighbor lists get updated for the new merged coalition $(C_i \cup C_j)$ and more possible merges are searched similarly till o more neighbors exists for a probable merge operation. The same process gets repeated for the remaining of the coalitions in partition $C = \{C_1, C_2, ..., C_s\}$ in absolute payoff value order as shown in Algorithm 1 till no more merges are possible. A new partition H is created after the merge operation is completed. Partition H is then subjected to split operation where each coalition H_i is verified for all the possible split choices and it's divided only if the total payoff of the split coalitions are better compared to the bigger coalition adopting the utilitarian order i.e. $\left(\sum_{j=1}^{y} u(H_{ij}) > u(H_i)\right)$. Split operation is then successively iterated for the remaining of the coalitions in partition H till there is no more split as given in Algorithm 2. Merge and split operations are then carried out iteratively till no more merge and split is done and the algorithm stops. The algorithm termination is always ensured since the objectives of all merge and split operations are the same i.e. improve the overall system utility u(C). There is always a definite number of merge/split operations possible for improving u(C) and the algorithm will stop when there is no possibility of increasing u(C) using merge/split operations.

Algorithm 1: Merge Operation

For any given network clustering state $C=\{C_1,C_2,...,C_s\}$, $\forall C_i \in C$, set C_i.Clustered=0

Merge-ongoing =1

While Merge-ongoing do

Merge-ongoing =0

Sort $\forall C_i \in C$ based on $u(C_i)$ in decreasing order

For all C_i where C_i.clustered=0 do

Update C_i.nei

For all $C_j$in C_i.nei where C_j.clustered=0 do

Update payoff gain for possible merge (C_i, C_j) i.e.

$$\delta_{u_{ij}} = u(C_i \cup C_j) - \{u(C_i) + u(C_j)\}$$

End for

Find $C_m \in C_i.nei$ where $\delta_{u_{im}} = \max_{C_j \in C_i, nei}(\delta_{u_{ij}})$ and $\delta_{u_{im}} > 0$

While C_m exist do

Merge (C_i, C_m)

C_m.clustered =1

Update C_i.nei

For all $C_j$in C_i.nei where C_j.clustered=0 do

Update payoff gain for possible merge (C_i, C_j)

i.e.$\delta_{u_{ij}} = u(C_i \cup C_j) - \{u(C_i) + u(C_j)\}$

End for

Find $C_m \in C_i.\mathrm{nei}$ where $\delta_{u_{im}} = \max_{C_j \in C_j,\mathrm{nei}}(\delta_{u_{ij}})$ and $\delta_{u_{im}} > 0$

End while

C_i.clustered=1

If any merge operation with C_i then

Break for-loop and continue with while-loop

Merge-ongoing=1

End if

End for

End while

Once a coalition is checked for a possible split and when no split operation is possible, then even if the re-clustering of the rest of the network is done, marked coalitions will not be verified again for split in the next iterations. Also, in this coalitional game framework, a soft maximum cluster size limit included in both utility functions is used to prevent the rise in signal processing and backhaul bandwidth necessary for collaboration. This constraint decreases the complexity on the split operation, i.e. less number of possible split choices exists owing to small cluster size. Also, the split operation ceases to search for other split choices if a split preference with better utility is got and therefore the split operation does not have to traverse through all the split choices in several scenarios.

Algorithm 2: Split Operation

For any given network clustering state $C=\{C_1, C_2,...,C_s\}$, $\forall C_i \in C$, set C_i.splitpossible = 1

Split-ongoing =1

While Split-ongoing do

Split-ongoing=0

For all C_i where (C_i.split-possible=1 and $|C_i|>1$) do

Update C_i.split-options

C_i.split-possible = 0

For all C_i.Split-possible =0

If any split option is possible i.e. $\left(\sum_{j=1}^{y} u(C_{ij}) > u(C_i)\right)$ then

Split (C_i to $\{C_{i1}, C_{i2},...,C_{iy}\}$)

Split-ongoing =1

$\forall C_{ij}$, set C_{ij}.split-possible=1

Break for-loop and continue with next C_i

End if

End for

End for

End while

To summarize, a low complexity merge and split operation is recommended in our novel game-theoretic clustering algorithm: The merge operations are limited to just neighbor clusters which increases the scalability of the solution and decreases the complexity. Also, a soft maximum cluster size constraint is included in both utility functions which decreases the complexity on split operation avoiding a higher number of probable splits.

5.5 TTL DECISION MAKING BASED ON NUMBER OF VEHICLES

The time-to-live (TTL) refers to the number of hops that a packet is allowed to traverse prior to being dropped by a router. The sending host specifies the TTL in an eight binary digit field in the packet header and is helpful in avoiding the packets from infinitely moving on the Internet or any other network. When an IP packet is forwarded, routers are needed to reduce the TTL by at least one. In case a packet's TTL field reaches zero, the router finding it drops the packet and transmits an ICMP (Internet control message protocol) message back to the host that originates it. The ping and the trace route utilities both use the TTL. The latter deliberately transmits the packets with less TTL values such that they will be dropped by every successive router present in the destination path. The time between transmitting a packet and receiving the ICMP message that it was dropped is considered for calculating the travel time for every successive hop. A particular TTL number can specify the maximum range for a packet. For instance, zero limits it to the same host, one to the same subnet, 32 to the same site, 64 to the same region and 128 to the same continent; 255 is unlimited. In this research work, TTL packet values are set depending on the number of vehicles existing in the cluster of coverage area. Therefore, the data communication can be successful.

For the explained technique, the messages present in the cache must be evenly disseminated. This distribution is automatically attained for information which the vehicles identify bypassing, since the vehicles are naturally driving over the road section one after another. But, when the vehicles are caught at the information location, every vehicle sends the information after detecting it and resends it once the TTL expires. This technique results in several messages quite concurrently. This problem is resolved through the addition of a random factor to the first retransmission interval. Rather than retransmitting after the TTL expires, the vehicle first retransmits after a ceratin time, which lies between 0 and the TTL T. In this manner, the messages distribution is more even.

5.6 RESULTS AND DISCUSSION

Experiments are carried out with 64 -bit Ubuntu 12.04 operating system, which includes Intel Core i7-2670QM processor @ 2.20 GHz and RAM of 8 GB. The network simulator tool utilized is NS2.34. The performance of the hybrid algorithm is evaluated by carrying out different experiments. Owing to the random quality of optimization algorithm, the algorithm is executed ten times and the result is evaluated with the average value. Table 5.1 gives simulation software parameters.

Table 5.1 Simulation software parameters

PRODUCTS	VALUE
Number of Vehicles	100 – 150
Dimension of simulation area	1000 X 1300 sq. meters
Simulation Time	150s
Physical layer Protocol	802.11p
Packet size	256 bytes
Data rate	4 Mbps
Number of lanes	2
Vehicle velocity	20-60 kmph
Number of Iteration	70

5.6.1 Simulation Results

The performance analysis of the discussed approach in terms of average throughput, routing overhead, delay and packet delivery ratio shown in Figures 5.1 – 5.4. The below Table 5.2 shows the packet delivery ratio values attained for the discussed and existing research approaches.

Table 5.2 Packet delivery ratio values

Number of vehicles	Methods		
	FCC-DRM	3 Stage fuzzy decision tree model	EcoTrec
100	69	53.3	49.2
110	80	56.4	53.7
120	89	69.6	62.9
130	91	72.5	67.6
140	93	74.1	71.3
150	94	79.55	73.2

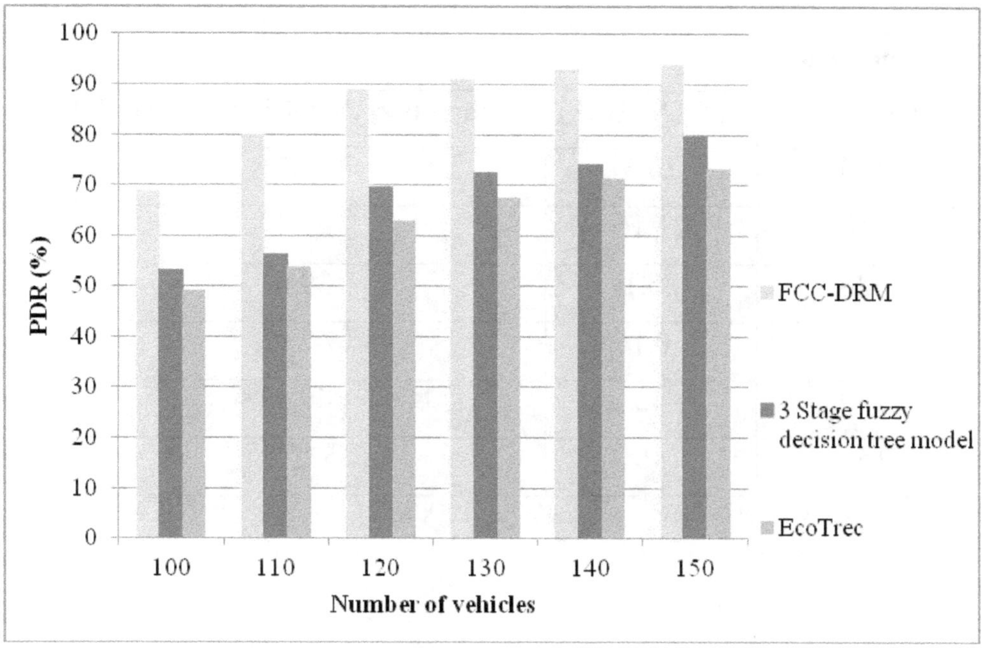

Figure 5.1 Packet Delivery Ratio Vs Number of vehicles

The effect of vehicle count on packet delivery ratio is shown in Figure 5.1 illustrates. PDR is defined as the ratio of packets count transmitted to the number of packets received. If there is an increase in the number of vehicles, PDR also rises. The plot clearly shows that the PDR is more in FCC-DRM scheme in comparison with the other approaches. It is proven from the graph that the proposed technique FCC-DRM yields 27.266% improved packet delivery ratio compared to 3 Stage fuzzy decision tree model and 36.54% improved packet delivery ratio compared to EcoTrec.

The below Table 5.3 shows the routing overhead values attained for the discussed and existing research approaches.

Table 5.3 Routing Overhead values

Number of vehicles	Methods		
	FCC-DRM	3 Stage fuzzy decision tree model	EcoTrec
100	20.3	23.3	25.6
110	22.16	26.4	27.9
120	25.1	39.6	42.4
130	30.16	42.9	45.6
140	42	49.4	53.2
150	46	52.52	55.4

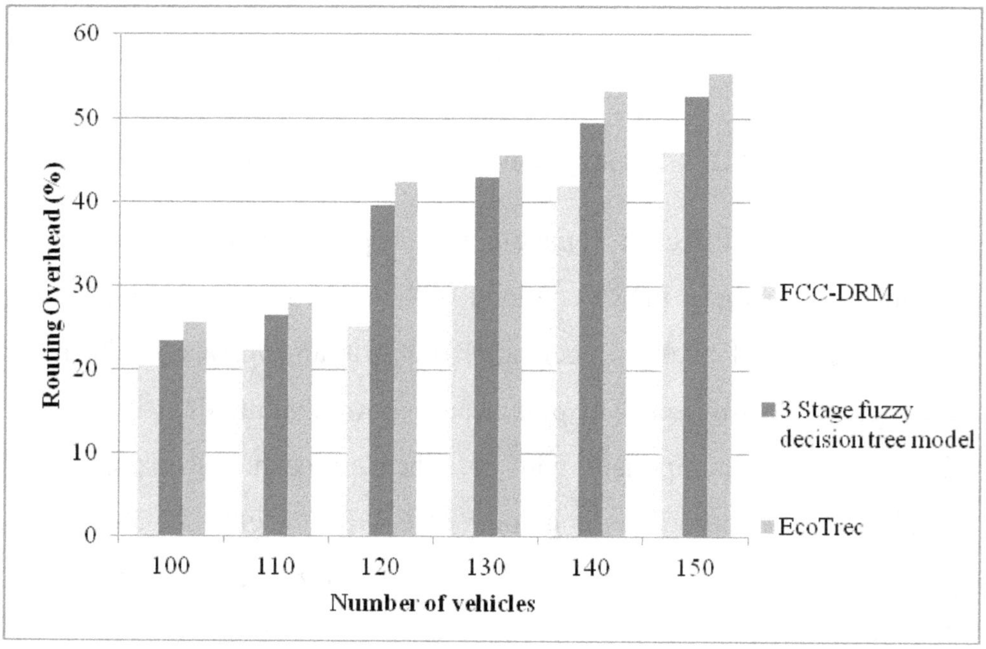

Figure 5.2 Routing overhead Vs Number of vehicles

The effect of the number of vehicles on the routing overhead is shown in Figure 5.2. Packets count distributed for each data packet indicates routing overhead. If the number of vehicles count increase, then there will be a rise in routing overhead. The packet loss is relatively low in the FCC-DRM approach. It is shown from this comparison that the proposed FCC-DRM reveals 20.67% decreased routing overhead compared to 3 stage fuzzy decision tree models and 25.74% decreased routing overhead compared to EcoTrec.

The below Table 5.4 shows the delay values attained for the discussed and existing research approaches.

Table 5.4 Delay values

Number of vehicles	Methods		
	FCC_DRM	3 Stage fuzzy decision tree model	EcoTrec
100	13	18	22
110	14	21	23
120	16	24	27
130	16.5	25	29
140	18	27	31
150	20	29	35

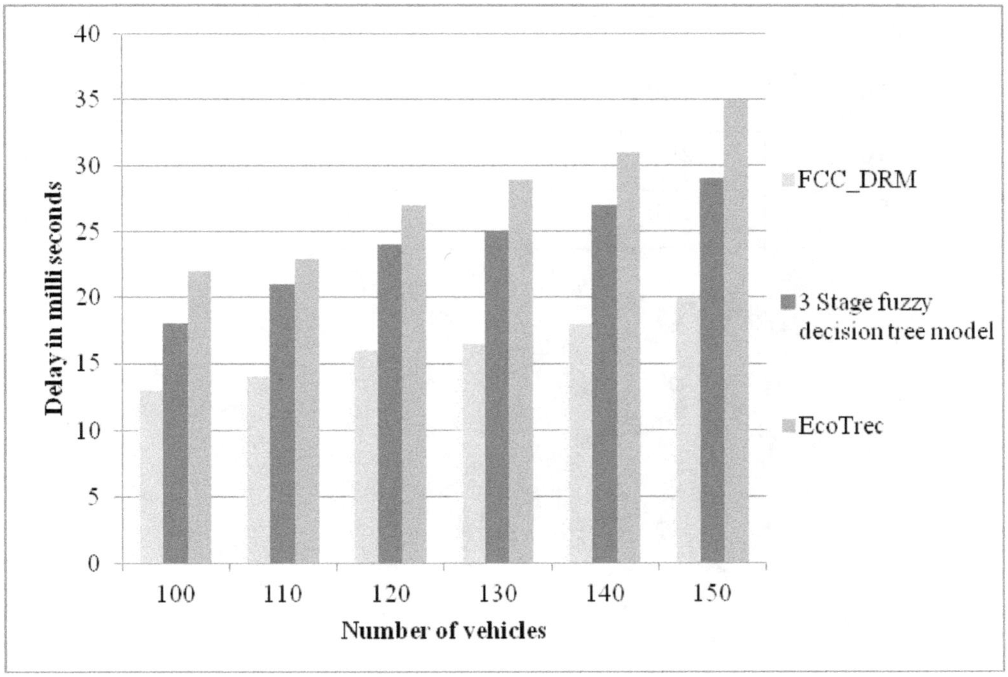

Figure 5.3 Delay Vs Number of vehicles

The effect of the number of vehicle on delay is shown in Figure 5.3. It is confirmed from this figure that the proposed techniques yields superior results with reduced delay that is comparatively better than the existing works like 3 Stage fuzzy decision tree model and EcoTrec. It is shown from this comparison that the proposed technique FCC-DRM yields 32.29% reduced delay compared to 3 stage fuzzy decision tree model and 41.61% reduced delay in EcoTrec.

The below Table 5.5 shows the throughput values attained for the discussed and existing research approaches.

Table 5.5 Throughput values

Number of vehicles	Techniques		
	FCC-DRM	3 Stage fuzzy decision tree model	EcoTrec
100	184	153.3	149.2
110	189	166.4	155.4
120	197	169.6	161.7
130	199	172.5	164.8
140	205	179.1	171.5
150	210	180.56	174.7

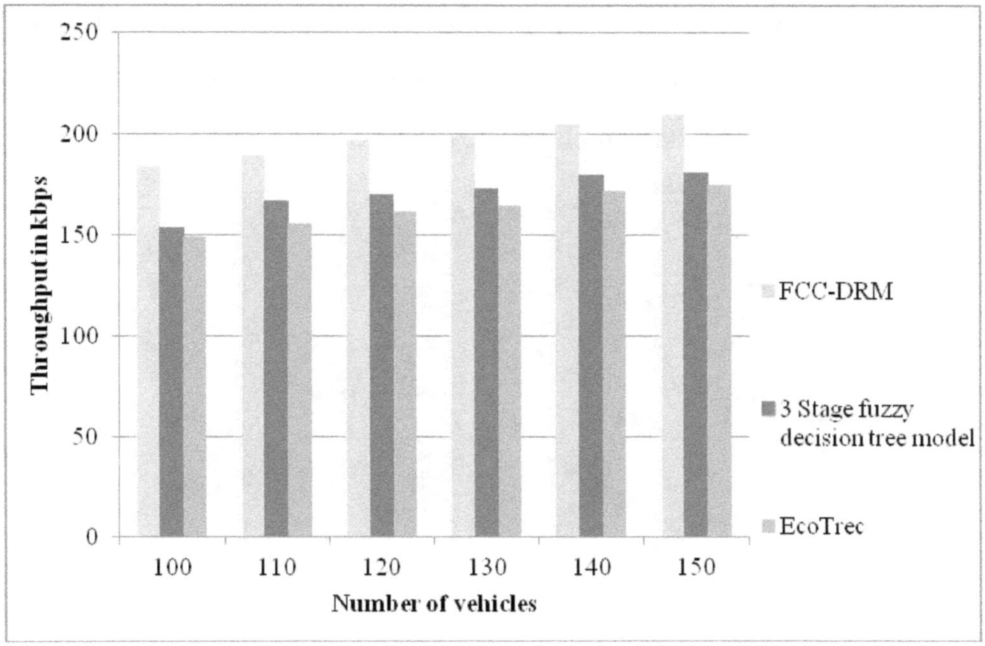

Figure 5.4 Average Throughput Vs Number of vehicles

The effect of the number of vehicles on average throughput is shown in Figure 5.4. Throughput defines the number of packets received successfully. Packet delivery rate is improved considerably in the proposed approach. It is noticed that the average throughput is high in FCC-DRM approach. It is proven from this comparison that the discussed FCC-DRM yields15.91% better throughput compared to 3 stage fuzzy decision tree model and 21.15% higher throughput compared to EcoTrec.

5.7 SUMMARY

This research work introduces Fuel Consumption and Coverage aware Dynamic Routing Model (FCC-DRM). To deal with the coverage control issues, in this stage, coverage and load aware clustering protocol is proposed. Also, the optimal cluster head selection is carried out by using the ant colony algorithm considering the parameters as follows. The parameters taken include Neighbour covered, Coverage redundancy, coverage area, connectivity factor. Depending on distance between the number of vehicles existing in the coverage area TTL of data is determined, and therefore a successful and rapid data transmission is ensured. This will result in lesser fuel consumption with good vehicle traffic control.

CHAPTER 6

RESULTS AND DISCUSSION

6.1 SIMULATION SETUP

An intuitive language, MATLAB offers a stretchy environment in computation technically that incorporates computation of mathematics and tools of visualization in data analysis for applications and algorithms development. Functions of 600 mathematical, statistical, and engineering features are focused. Its open architecture and companion products allow users to explore, develop, share and modify data sets, algorithms and custom tools, thereby achieving a fairly fast updating, improving and expanding of the MATLAB environment.

MATLAB (MATrix LABoratory) is a numerical computing environment and fourth-generation programming language. Developed by Math Works, MATLAB allows matrix manipulations, plotting of functions and data, implementation of algorithms, creation of user interfaces, and interfacing with programs written in other languages, including C, C++, Java, and FORTRAN. Although MATLAB is intended primarily for numerical computing, an optional toolbox uses the MuPAD symbolic engine, allowing access to symbolic computing capabilities. An additional package, Simulink, adds graphical multi-domain simulation and Model-Based Design for dynamic and embedded systems. In 2004, MATLAB had around one million users across industry and academia. MATLAB users come from various backgrounds of engineering, science, and economics. MATLAB is widely used in academic and research institutions as well as industrial enterprises.

The MATLAB application is built around the MATLAB language. The simplest way to execute MATLAB code is to type it in the Command Window, which is one of the elements of the MATLAB Desktop. When code is entered in the Command Window, MATLAB can be used as an interactive mathematical shell. Sequences of commands can be saved in a text file, typically using the MATLAB Editor, as a script or encapsulated into a function, extending the commands available.

6.1.1 MATLAB Features

- Simple programming environment including control structures like loops and selections.
- Linear algebraic system solvers for vectors, matrices and functionality like computing products and inverses, scaling, summing, multiplications, factorizations, and so on.
- Simple graphic interface for visualization and simulation. Open component system based on toolboxes which can be created, modified, customized and shared by the users.
- High-level language for technical computing Development environment for managing code, files, and data Interactive tools for iterative exploration, design, and problem solving Mathematical functions for linear algebra, statistics, Fourier analysis, filtering, optimization, and numerical integration 2-D and 3-D graphics functions for visualizing data Tools for building custom graphical user interfaces .Functions for integrating MATLAB based algorithms with external applications and languages, such as C, C++, Fortran, Java, COM, and Microsoft Excel Development Environment(5:02)

- Ability to zip and unzip files and folders in the Current Folder browser to simplify sharing of files
- New visual cues in the Current Folder browser to show directories on the MATLAB path
- Enhanced tab completion in the MATLAB Editor with support for local variables, sub functions, and nested functions
- Expanded access in the plot selector to plots from the Curve Fitting, Filter Design, Image Processing, and Signal Processing Toolboxes
- Enhanced File and Folder Comparison Tool, highlighting changes within lines in file comparisons, and sorting results by name, type, size, or timestamp in folder comparisons Performance and Large Data Set Handling
- Multithreaded computation support for long vector fft, conv2, integer conversion, and integer arithmetic functions
- Performance improvements for mrdivide, convn, histc, sortrows, and sparse matrix indexed assignment

6.1.2 Advantages of Matlab

- Low time consumption in MATLAB. After only a few hours of training, a new MATLAB user can start developing simulation tools.
- Recent versions of the MATLAB compiler can compile to C, C++ and binary code, allowing the use of different optimization options for high-speed executables.
- As a consequence, performance of the MATLAB linear-algebraic solvers has been drastically improved in the latest versions of the

software, which include also additional accelerators for operations with vector/matrix data types.

- The open architecture allows for very rapid extension of the range of functionality of MATLAB by developing and sharing new toolboxes.
- Using MATLAB tools and toolboxes, it is possible to develop a prototype of an application for a relatively very short time.

It is easy to exchange toolboxes and parts of code within a team and between teams working in the same area.

6.2 NUMERICAL ANALYSIS

Experimentation is done using 64 -bit Ubuntu 12.04 operating system having Intel Core i7-2670QM processor @ 2.20 GHz and RAM of 8 GB. The network simulator tool used is NS2.34. The performance of the hybrid algorithm is analyzed by conducting various experiments. Due to stochastic quality of optimization algorithm, the algorithm is executed ten times and the result is analyzed with the average value. Table 6.1 provides simulation software parameters.

Table 6.1 Simulation software parameters

PRODUCT	VALUE
Number of Vehicles	100 – 150
Dimension of simulation area	1000 X 1300 sq. meters
Simulation Time	150s
Physical layer Protocol	802.11p
Packet size	256 bytes
Data rate	4 Mbps
Number of lanes	2
Vehicle velocity	20-60 kmph
Number of Iteration	70

6.2.1 Simulation Results

The performance analysis of proposed technique with respect to average throughput, routing overhead, delay and packet delivery ratio is illustrated in Figures 6.1 – 6.4.

In the following Table 6.2, packet delivery ratio values obtained for the proposed and existing research techniques has been shown.

Table 6.2 Packet delivery ratio values

Number of vehicles	Methods				
	FCC-DRM	FCD - TSM	RG technique	3 Stage fuzzy decision tree model	EcoTrec
100	69	62.4	57	53.3	49.2
110	80	69.88	62	56.4	53.7
120	89	73.67	70	69.6	62.9
130	91	75.3	73.6	72.5	67.6
140	93	76.5	75.2	74.1	71.3
150	94	82.7	80.11	79.55	73.2

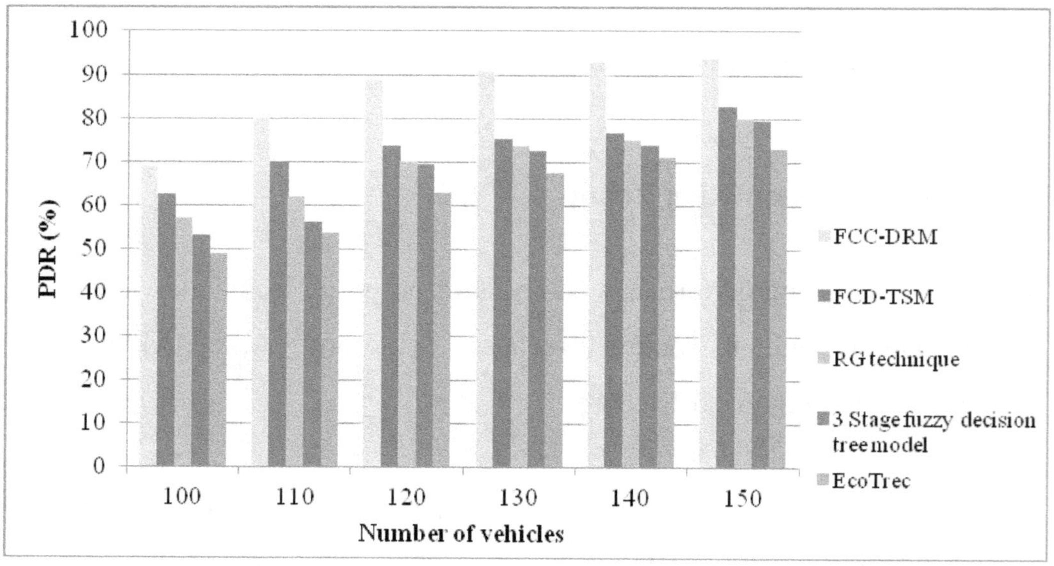

Figure 6.1 Packet Delivery Ratio Vs Number of vehicles

The vehicle count influence on packet delivery ratio was shown in Figure 6.1. PDR is a ratio of packets count sent to packets count received. When vehicles count increases, PDR also increases. Plot clearly illustrates that the PDR is higher in FCC-DRM approach compared to the other techniques. As the clear routing part is construction From the graphical comparison it is confirmed that the proposed method FCC-DRM shows 17.15% increased packet delivery ration than FCD-TSM, 23.47% increased packet delivery ration than RG technique, 27.266% increased packet delivery ratio than 3 Stage fuzzy decision tree model and 36.54% increased packet delivery ratio than EcoTrec.

In the following Table 6.3, routing overhead values obtained for the proposed and existing research techniques has been shown.

Table 6.3 Routing Overhead values

Number of vehicles	Methods				
	FCC-DRM	FCD-TSM	RG technique	3 Stage fuzzy decision tree model	EcoTrec
100	20.3	22.4	22.9	23.3	25.6
110	22.16	25.88	26.2	26.4	27.9
120	25.1	27.67	31.54	39.6	42.4
130	30.16	35.3	39.65	42.9	45.6
140	42	46.5	47.84	49.4	53.2
150	46	48.7	51.05	52.52	55.4

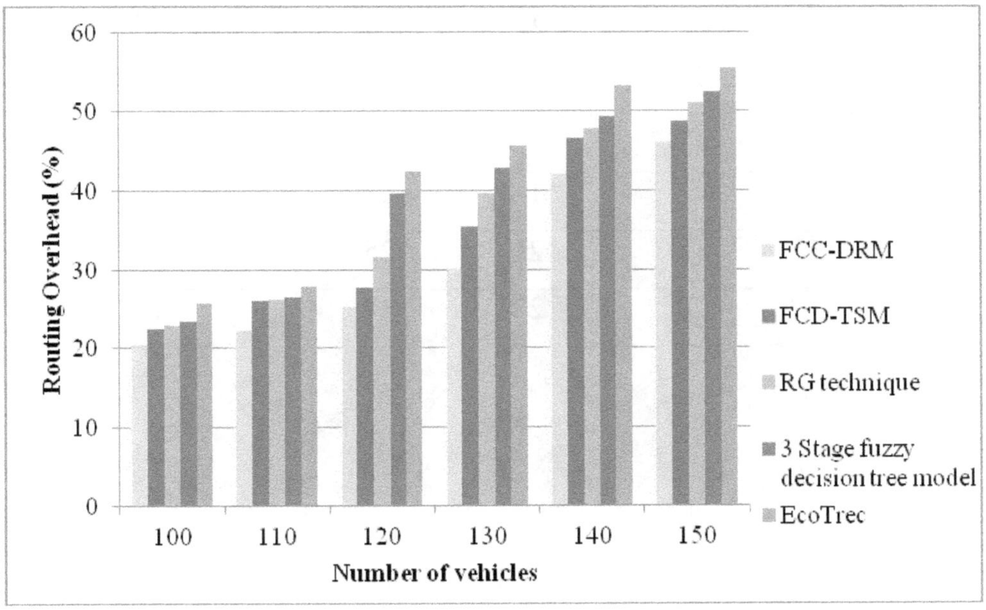

Figure 6.2 Routing overhead Vs Number of vehicles

The influence of the number of vehicles and the routing overhead was shown in Figure 6.2. Packets count distributed per data packet specifies routing overhead. When vehicles count increases there will be an increase in routing overhead. The packet loss is comparatively lesser in the FCC-DRM technique. From this comparison it is confirmed that the proposed FCC-DRM shows 10.04% reduced routing overhead than FCD-TSM, 15.26% reduced routing overhead than RG technique, 20.67% reduced routing overhead than 3 stage fuzzy decision tree model and 25.74% reduced routing overhead than EcoTrec.

In the following Table 6.4, delay values obtained for the proposed and existing research techniques has been shown.

Table 6.4 Delay values

Number of vehicles	**Methods**				
	FCC_DRM	**FCD-TSM**	**RG technique**	**3 Stage fuzzy decision tree model**	**EcoTrec**
100	13	15	16	18	22
110	14	15.5	17	21	23
120	16	17	19	24	27
130	16.5	18	22	25	29
140	18	21	25	27	31
150	20	23	27	29	35

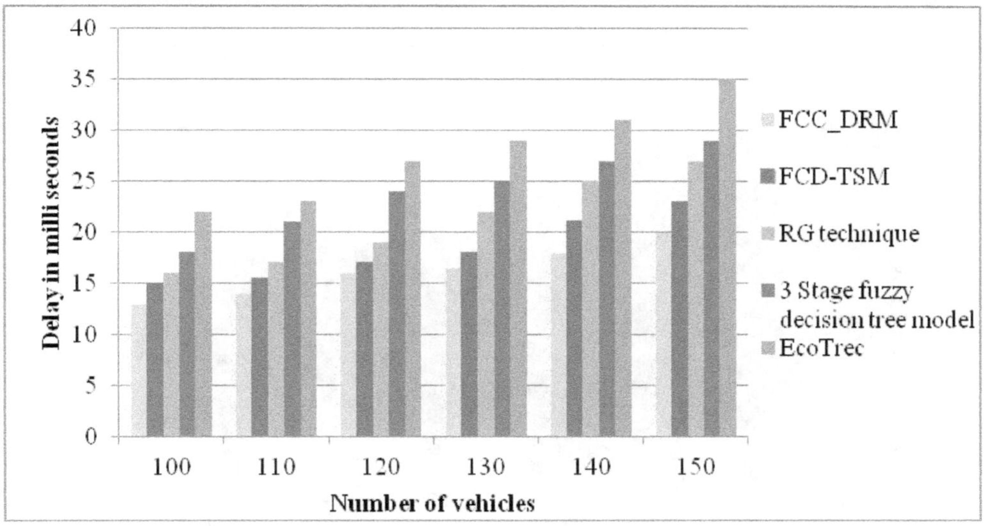

Figure 6.3 Delay Vs Number of vehicles

The vehicle counts impact and delay was shown in Figure 6.3. From this figure it is proved that the proposed methods tends to have better outcome with lesser delay which is considerably better than the existing work 3 Stage fuzzy decision tree model and EcoTrec. From this comparison it is proved that the proposed method FCC-DRM shows 10.95% lesser delay than FCD-TSM, 22.6% lesser delay than RG technique, 32.29% lesser delay than 3 stage fuzzy decision tree model and 41.61% lesser delay in EcoTrec.

In the following Table 6.5, throughput values obtained for the proposed and existing research techniques has been shown.

Table 6.5 Throughput values

Number of vehicles	Methods				
	FCC-DRM	FCD-TSM	RG technique	3 Stage fuzzy decision tree model	EcoTrec
100	184	172.4	165	153.3	149.2
110	189	179.81	172	166.4	155.4
120	197	183.67	175	169.6	161.7
130	199	195.3	183	172.5	164.8
140	205	196.5	189	179.1	171.5

150	210	192.7	191	180.56	174.7

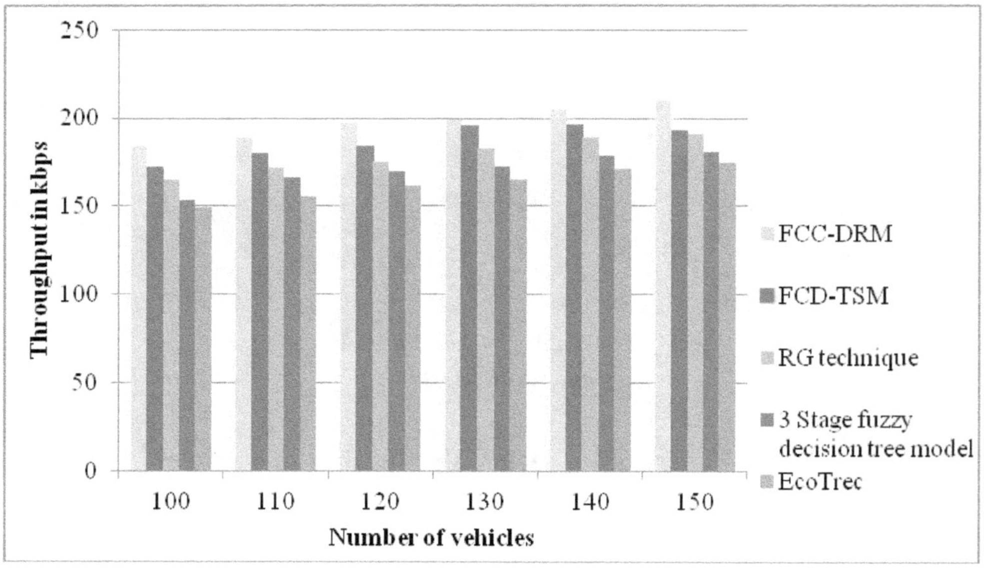

Figure 6.4 Average Throughput Vs Number of vehicles

The vehicle counts impact and average throughput was shown in Figure 6.4. The number of successful reception of packets defines throughput. Packet delivery rate is increased relatively in the proposed technique. It is observed that the average throughput is more in FCC-DRM technique. From this comparison it is confirmed that the proposed FCC-DRM shows 5.67% higher throughput than FCD-TSM, 10.13% higher throughput than RG technique, 15.91% higher throughput than 3 stage fuzzy decision tree model and 21.15% higher throughput than EcoTrec.

CHAPTER 7

CONCLUSION AND FUTURE WORK

7.1 CONCLUSION

In real time vehicular ADHOC network environment, fuel consumption reduction is the more important problem which is focused in this research work. In this research fuel consumption reduction is guaranteed by reducing the waiting time of vehicles in the road traffic by making accurate and faster decision regarding traffic management.

In the first research work proposed a Finite automata model for the design of our VANET. Using that model, various formulas are developed for calculating the fuel consumed by various vehicles, CO_2 emission from various vehicles, and the traffic reduction during peak hour. Fuel, CO_2 and traffic level are also be calculated in weekly basis.

In the second research work Fuel Consumption and Delay aware Traffic Scheduling Method (FCD-TSM) is introduced. To support the vehicles with different transmission ranges and sensitivity in this work coverage aware clustering is done in which VANET nodes will be grouped together through which faster data communication can be ensured. To ensure the successful data transmission and guaranteeing accurate decision making, in this work message replication quota is decided according to nodes count in cluster, which reduce the network load and ensures the successful data transmission.

In the third research work Fuel Consumption and Coverage aware Dynamic Routing Model (FCC-DRM) is introduced. To balance the coverage control problems, in this phase coverage and load aware clustering protocol is introduced. Here, the optimal cluster head selection is performed by introducing the Ant Colony Algorithm with the consideration of following parameters. The parameters that are considered are Neighbour covered, Coverage redundancy, Coverage area and Connectivity factor. Based on distance between the number of vehicles present in the coverage area TTL of data is decided, thus the successful and faster data transmission is guaranteed. This will lead to reduced fuel consumption with proper vehicle traffic management.

In MATLAB environment, evaluation of this research work is done and better results are exhibited by proposed work when compared with existing work as shown by results of experimentation.

7.2 FUTURE WORK

Selfish nodes and malicious nodes present in the VANET environment might lead to the inefficient VANET routing and increased fuel consumption. In future scenario, it is required to consider avoidance of selfish nodes to improvise the overall network performance.

The computation overhead of the research work is higher which needs to be handled in future by introducing the unwanted control message avoidance.

In future, it is required to consider the presence of uncooperative nodes present in the VANET environment to improvise the overall network performance.

www.ingramcontent.com/pod-product-compliance
Lightning Source LLC
LaVergne TN
LVHW082344200926
848481LV00012B/3445

* 9 7 9 8 2 3 1 7 0 5 4 6 7 *